MegaSkills®

for Babies, Toddlers, and Beyond

MegaSkills®

for Babies, Toddlers, and Beyond

Building Your Child's Happiness and Success for Life

Dorothy Rich, EdD, and Beverly Mattox, MEd

Foreword by Marguerite Kelly, syndicated parenting columnist
and co-author, *The Mother's Almanac*

SOURCEBOOKS, INC.®
NAPERVILLE, ILLINOIS

Published by Sourcebooks, Inc.
P.O. Box 4410, Naperville, Illinois 60567–4410
(630) 961–3900
Fax: (630) 961–2168
www.sourcebooks.com

Library of Congress Cataloging-in-Publication Data

Rich, Dorothy.
  Megaskills for babies, toddlers, and beyond : building your child's happiness and success for life / by Dorothy Rich and Beverly Mattox.
       p. cm.
  1. Child rearing. 2. Education—Parent participation. 3. Success in children. I. Mattox, Beverly A. II. Title.
  HQ769.R467 2009
  649'.68—dc22

                                       2008008722

                          Printed and bound in Canada
                          TR 10 9 8 7 6 5 4 3 2 1

MegaSkills for Babies, Toddlers, and Beyond
is dedicated to all who nurture the very
best in our children and in ourselves.

Also by Dorothy Rich: **The MegaSkills® Series**

MegaSkills: How Families Can Help Children Succeed in School and Beyond

MegaSkills: The Best Gift You Can Give Your Child

MegaSkills: Building Children's Achievement for the Information Age

Career MegaSkills: Habits, Attitudes, and Behaviors for Doing Well in School and on the Job

Also by Beverly Mattox:

Getting It Together: Dilemmas for the Classroom Based on Kohlberg's Approach

101 Activities for Building More Effective School-Community Involvement, co-authored with Dorothy Rich

Contents

Foreword

All parents want their children to be confident, caring, and respectful of others, and to be motivated, focused, and responsible, too, not just when they're young but for the rest of their lives. And that's not all. They want them to learn whatever they can, whenever they can, and then to mix this information with their own ideas and a healthy dash of common sense, so they will dare to work hard and long to solve a problem, even when the odds are tough and their teammates are more difficult than they should be.

Many children reach most of these goals and a few children reach all of them but no child reaches any of them completely on his own—and neither will yours. It takes the guidance of a parent, a grandparent, a teacher, or even the old lady next door to open a child's eyes to the pleasure of giving; the beauty of nature; the orderliness of science, mathematics, and music; and the building of words and colors into stories and pictures—as well as the survival skills that make life so much easier and more pleasant.

Your child will notice and probably appreciate some of these things, whether he has any guidance or not, but if someone doesn't encourage his curiosity, his work ethic, and his character, his full potential will be pruned away by the sharp and careless shears of inaction.

This doesn't mean that you should rush out and enroll your baby in a gym class or find someone to teach your two-year-old how to cook or paint or study the stars; not at all. As Dorothy Rich discovered in her fine MegaSkills program, even a very young child can learn about the wonders of the world just by the directions he gets when he plays in the kitchen, the garden, the workshop, and even the bathtub.

That is the value of this book: a when-to, why-to guide to teach parents how to explain both the tangible and the intangible rudiments of life to children before they ever start school, for these are the years when they soak up information osmotically.

These are also the years when parents discover that the more their children learn, the more they want to learn.

The child who helps to measure the half-teaspoon of mustard and the cup of olive oil is getting an early lesson in fractions. The child who is told that mustard and oil can emulsify but mustard and vinegar cannot will remember it much better if she's first allowed to mix the mustard with the vinegar, to see that these ingredients will never blend, and then to mix the mustard with the oil.

It may seem boring for you to teach this—or any of life's little lessons—to your child after spending a long day at the office, and sometimes it may seem like the last straw, but these lessons are just that: little, both in time and in effort. It only takes five to seven minutes to whip up a week's supply of vinaigrette, even if your child is helping you.

And so it is when you plant tulips together, letting your child measure the holes you did for each bulb, to make sure that they are five inches deep. You wouldn't go to that trouble yourself, but it's a quick way to teach your child about inches and it gives you something interesting to talk about.

MegaSkills is a matter of giving children the attention they need at the time they need it, and in the way they need it, too.

Much depends on how you communicate with your children. The more you talk *with* them instead of *at* them, the better they will listen and the more they will learn. What are small tasks to you are fascinating challenges to them, giving them the kind of information they will think about for weeks and years to come.

Children need to learn their numbers and letters in kindergarten, of course, but first they need to learn how to do many small jobs and why, just as they need to move their arms and legs quite well before their fingers are adept enough to write those numbers and letters.

To emphasize the academics without giving a child the basics first is like telling him to climb a ladder that has lost its first few rungs. They won't do their schoolwork as well; they won't have that broad basis of knowledge that all children deserve, and they won't be as competent—and therefore as confident—as nature meant for them to be.

Your children aren't the only ones who lose, however, if you don't teach them all the little things you know. You too will lose, for the small skills you teach your children will give great satisfaction to you now and it will turn the family into a team later, because each one of you will be doing your part. Nothing makes a child feel better than to be needed—and nothing relieves a parent more than to count on the children to do their share, as best they can.

—Marguerite Kelly, syndicated parenting columnist
and co-author, *The Mother's Almanac*

What This Book Is About and Why It's Important

1

"The child supplies the power, but the parents have to do the steering."
— Benjamin Spock

When parents and teachers across the world are asked what they want for their children, their answers center on the cornerstones of character and achievement: responsibility, dependability, curiosity, eagerness to learn, self-discipline, sensitivity to others, and willingness to work hard. So, where are the "recipes" to teach these attitudes and behaviors? *They are here, in this book.*

Everyone says our kids have to know more. To try to make this happen, preschool and school curriculums are being pushed down from first grade to kindergarten, some from third grade to first. This is the wrong way to go. Sure, many of our children can learn more than they are currently learning, but driving the usual curriculum down younger and younger is not a winning solution. Using traditional curricula keyed to test scores ignores the basic prerequisites for character and achievement that our kids need to learn at home.

That's what this book offers—the basics that can be learned easily and naturally before children are school age, so that when they go to school, they go with abilities well beyond the alphabet and counting to ten.

Having taught MegaSkills to school age children for over twenty years, we have been urged to create MegaSkills for children starting at age one and moving to school entry. This program is not designed to create "little Einsteins." It is designed to create curious, positive learners. *MegaSkills for Babies, Toddlers, and Beyond* is the result of our tested experience and is a response to children's learning needs today, which are greater than the learning needs of yesterday.

• Getting Started

Every child is entitled to know what it takes to succeed; yet many children today are deprived of this birthright. Many of our children come into classrooms not knowing what it is to be responsible, not really knowing what it means to be persevering, and what it is to use common sense.

The good news is that these basics can be taught and they can be taught in children's very early years. MegaSkills are not "drill and kill" early academics. MegaSkills teach the habits, behaviors, and attitudes that children need early in life, throughout the school years and beyond.

• What are MegaSkills?

MegaSkills are the *superbasics*. They are the prerequisites that make it possible for us to learn everything else.

MEGASKILLS

Confidence	Feeling able to do it
Motivation	Wanting to do it
Effort	Being willing to work hard
Responsibility	Doing what's right
Initiative	Moving into action
Perseverance	Completing what you start
Caring	Showing concern for others
Teamwork	Working with others
Common Sense	Using good judgment
Problem Solving	Putting what you know and what you can do into action
Focus	Concentrating with a goal in mind
Respect	Showing good behavior, courtesy, and appreciation

MegaSkills are our "inner engines of learning." We all know they are important. They can and must be taught in order to build a child's ability to learn.

• *The Special Importance of MegaSkills Today*

Our world is increasingly complex, with more information and more technology to learn. The influence of television, computers, and peer pressure has increased, and the family is under greater time constraints.

The "Three Rs" are still needed—but they are no longer enough. Students need to be prepared for the world of work in a more competitive twenty-first century, which is a major impetus behind the drive for school reform. Studies report that the desire to learn, the ability to function cooperatively, the capacity to concentrate, the motivation to do well, and, above all, the self-discipline to keep learning are the attributes most strongly needed today. These are truly the "new basics." They are built incrementally, from the early years on.

Educational reform starts at home. Yes, schools have a big job to do, and many need to be doing a better job. But the current reform emphasis in education is far too narrow. The reform vision has to be broadened so that it includes families and communities. And it all has to start well before the traditional school years.

Mounting research indicates that family involvement in a child's education leads to higher achievement and improved school performance. Findings on crime and drugs point to the central preventive role of the family. The business world has identified education as a top priority to ensure its competitive future and that of the nation.

These are not insurmountable challenges. But, they require redirection of our thinking about how to improve education. From our own earliest work in teaching, it was clear to us that the important educational responsibilities of the home were being overlooked. Experience confirms that intellectual achievement is determined to a great extent by student emotions, motivation, and commitment.

Students need and don't get enough active, hands-on learning. That's why we created learning recipes—easy, at-home activities that teach complex content. Learning recipes are like what you find in cookbooks, except that our activities show you how to use a rug to encourage math, a clock to teach reading, and the bathtub to teach science. These activities are different from school-based lessons on purpose. These recipes work. Families get involved and children succeed.

• *The Theory Behind Learning Recipes*

When we started our work in education, we had five big questions. Ever since, we have been trying to find the answers:

- What is it that enables every child to achieve in school and in life?

- What can every parent do to help?

- What can every teacher do?

- How can we be more democratic and give every child a better chance at success?

- And perhaps most significant, what is it in our education work that we have been overlooking, not doing, or not doing enough?

As we continued teaching and gained more experience, we became convinced that good education is a continuing collaboration between home and school. And this starts early. Today, as we review almost fifty years of work since we began asking those questions, what emerges is lots of action and an underlying philosophy about what it means to teach and learn.

MegaSkills Instructional Principles

The learning recipes in this book have been designed to provide a variety of learning experiences within a consistent format. They help children become more aware of their own behaviors and attitudes, better able to express themselves, and able to gain more productive attitudes, behaviors, and habits for building later school achievement. They also provide opportunities for enjoyable learning: creativity, drawing, problem solving, and decision making.

In addition, the recipes include a variety of experiences for visual, auditory, and kinesthetic learning. While useful for all children, multidimensional learning experiences are particularly helpful for children with special learning needs. There are also many opportunities for children to work together with parents and friends to increase social skills.

Feminine and masculine pronouns are used interchangeably throughout. MegaSkills are vital for both boys and girls.

About Students

We believe that the key factor that makes students study hard and stay in school is a "C" word—*caring,* not *curriculum*. Students have to feel needed. That is the human element in education. Caring and connectedness are protective factors in our lives. That's why we looked for and developed ways to help students (and parents, regardless of background and income) to feel connected to education. Students need a home life that values learning as well as parents/caregivers who know how to provide practical support.

About Teachers

Human emotions and attitudes matter so much in teaching and learning that they can override the best lesson plan. For parents and teachers, this makes problem-solving attitudes and student motivation paramount. For students, taking responsibility and making an effort are central.

One education myth that remains strong, despite all that is known about the intricacies of learning, is that somehow learning is a straight line: a teacher teaches, a student learns. In actuality, education is a slow, messy, zigzag process. Teachers must learn to be resilient and be able to encourage themselves as well as the children they work with.

About Parents/Caregivers

The overwhelming majority of a child's learning time is spent outside the school. At best, students go to school half the days of the year and stay only about one-quarter of each day. These numbers alone ought to convince school boards, parents, and politicians that not everything that's important to learning is taking place in school. Yet recent legislation—both federal and state—continues to support the myth of the school as an all-powerful institution and pays little attention to the learning that takes place in the home and community. This book focuses on this out-of-school learning.

The adults in a child's life must send a clear message that education is important and that children can and will achieve. Adults need not be graduates of fancy colleges or have high incomes to be able to help children learn. Every parent and every caregiver is a teacher, and every day and every place is a learning opportunity.

• MegaSkills Impact: The Evidence That It Works

Parents and teachers have been sharing their success stories with us for many years. MegaSkills has proven to be a winner for children and families and teachers. For the evaluation data, see the studies in Appendix E.

2

Getting Started

"MegaSkills has been a lifesaver for our whole family"
— MegaSkills Mom

MegaSkills for Babies, Toddlers, and Beyond is the first book of its kind specifically designed for the early years (ages one through six), addressing the academic and character development balance that is necessary for childhood achievement. We have included more than two hundred easy-to-do home activities that uniquely use everyday routines for teaching the values and abilities parents want for their children. Our approach is that by starting early with your child, you can go well beyond the alphabet and numbers to teach vital attitudes and behaviors. Here is a brief explanation of how this book is organized.

There are seven MegaSkills chapters, organized by age category. Each chapter contains activities for the twelve MegaSkills, from Confidence to Respect, and are further broken down by developmental theme. There are six flexible age categories plus a chapter of activities for children who need more practice.

In addition, there are technology tips for parents, as well as MegaSkills Measures for parents and children, more resources, and a specially compiled list of children's books that support the MegaSkills values.

• *Where Do I Start?*

Activities throughout the book supplement and expand on each other, in order to provide more experience with activities that children particularly enjoy. Children love to duplicate and repeat what they enjoy and have learned.

Specific developmental themes are provided for each activity. These are:

- **Connect with Others**
- **Create and Imagine**
- **Personal Competency**
- **Listen, Speak, and Do**
- **Pre-Read and Respond**
- **Promote Good Daily Habits**
- **Reach Out and Explore**
- **Think and Organize**

Your Child's First MegaSkills: Approximate Ages and Stages

The activities range from easy to more challenging, and there are no hard and fast age distinctions. Many young children will enjoy activities planned for an older age group and vice versa. Remember that children develop at their own pace and in their own ways. Here are the ages and stages we've identified for this book:

Starting Out:	Children one to two years old
Keeping Going:	Children two to three years old
Sailing Along:	Children more advanced at a two or three year stage
Moving Forward:	Children three to four years old
Taking Big Steps:	Children four to five years old
Opening School Doors:	Children five to six years old
Look, Listen, and Do:	Activities for children who need more practice

• How to Choose MegaSkills Activities

Identify a MegaSkill your child needs to build and pick a Developmental Theme. Choose activities from any chapter. Every child is an individual and different activities will work at different ages.

Let's say your child is between the ages of one and two and you want to strengthen physical and motor skills. First, check the list of activities that begins each chapter. Developmental Themes are noted for each activity. One that may be helpful to you and your child is "Reach Out and Explore." Determine which activities appeal to you and your child and get started.

Let's say your child is between the ages of two and three and you want to encourage stronger language development. There are two sets of activities for ages two to three, "Keeping Going" and "Sailing Along." In both you will find activities focusing on the Developmental Theme of "Listen, Speak, and Do." Determine which activities appeal to you and your child and get started.

Let's say your child is between the ages of four and five and needs practice in doing what has to be done. Check the chapter and look at activities that "Promote Good Daily Habits."

If your child is between the ages of five and six and is getting ready for school, check out activities that help children "Think and Organize."

You get the idea. On each of the chapter contents pages, the MegaSkill and the Developmental Theme are listed next to the activity name.

• *Research Findings Tell Us*

"Most parents watch proudly as their five-year-old grabs that backpack and heads out the door to the first day of kindergarten—their 'official' start into the world of education and learning. Few imagine that their child has been preparing for school many years.

"Children are born ready to learn. Children are naturally curious beings who are motivated to make sense of the world around them. The brain is the only organ that is not fully formed at birth. During the first three years, trillions of connections between brain cells are being made. Children's relationships and experiences during their early years greatly influence how their brains grow.

"Children learn best through everyday experiences with the people they love and trust, and when the learning is fun."—Zero to Three (www.zerotothree.com; used with permission)

• Love and Economics

We all want to give our children a leg up without pushing them over. We want to give our children advantages that we may or may not have had. The strongest advantage every child can have is education. *MegaSkills for Babies, Toddlers, and Beyond* builds that education base. It starts early, easily, and without pressure. With MegaSkills, our children will be ready.

3

Understanding MegaSkills

"If you want your children to keep their feet on the ground, put some responsibility on their shoulders."
—Abigail Van Buren, "Dear Abby"

• About the MegaSkill Confidence: Feeling Able to Do It

We may be born with confidence, but we also lose it. Then we rebuild it again. It's like an ongoing construction project. And it's also like a wave—it ebbs and flows. A good thing happens and we feel more confident. Then, a not-so-good thing happens, and we lose that confident feeling. We know what we're hearing when a child says: "I can't do that." "The other kids are better than I am." "I'm scared." "I won't try it." We're hearing a child's cry for more confidence. It cuts to the heart.

Self-esteem is important, but it is a hollow concept unless it is based on experience. Self-esteem is not a separate "course." It's part of daily life, a result of ongoing, achievement-building activity. We help children develop confidence by providing opportunities to have successful experiences at home. These experiences need to be small enough for a child to handle, large enough to really give the message "I can do it!" and easy enough for parents to work with. It's important for parents to tell children they are capable, but to feel truly confident, children need to *experience* their own successes.

> *Look for Confidence-Building Activities in this book to answer this question for the years ahead: How can I help my child gain the courage to say "I can" instead of "I can't"?*

• *About the MegaSkill Motivation: Wanting to Do It*

We are born learners. The baby who reaches out to pull at our hair and who pushes things off the table is reaching out to the world, to find out how things work. If we could bottle this motivation from early childhood, repackage it for our growing-up years and hold on to it, then motivation for our children as they grow would not be a problem. But holding onto it is a challenge and a problem. Early motivation needs to be replenished as the years pass, and it needs to be reconfigured for the growing years.

In this age of fast-paced entertainment, where the media advertises that the action never stops, it can be hard for children to tolerate the moments in their own lives when the action does stop. It can get very easy for a child to say, "I'm bored," and for parents to somehow feel a twinge of guilt and frustration about it. Forget this guilt. We cannot be motivated for our children, and we can't keep them from feeling bored, if that is what they want to feel. The best we can do—and it's a lot—is to help children take charge of their own motivation and to see their own responsibility for being interested and motivated.

Look for Motivation-Building Activities in this book to answer this question for the years ahead: How can I help my child keep interested in learning and keep him from saying those dreaded words, "I'm bored"?

• *About the MegaSkill Effort: Being Willing to Work Hard*

Effort gets things done. It has the added benefit of making us feel good. We feel satisfaction. That's the beauty of effort. We look for ways to be more in charge of our responsibilities, rather than having them in charge of us.

Effort also has its secrets. The child learning magic tricks, the adult perfecting a golf game or struggling with a crossword puzzle, the tennis enthusiast practicing strokes over and over, the aspiring figure skater at the rink at dawn, the marathon runner who practically drops before stopping—these are people making lots of effort. They think they are enjoying themselves. It feels like enjoyment. The secret is that it is. In sports, people expend enormous effort without having it feel like effort at all. And it doesn't seem to matter, because it's effort that feels like pleasure.

Even young children know what it means to work hard. When kindergartners are asked to describe effort, they talk about taking care of pets, getting involved in sports, and doing chores around the house. When they are asked to describe what it means to be lazy, they also have no problem. They speak of sitting in front of the TV and not doing their chores. In short, children understand effort.

Look for Effort-Building Activities in this book to answer this question for the years ahead: How can I help my child tackle hard jobs without thinking they are too tough to handle?

• About the MegaSkill Responsibility: Doing What's Right

Some responsibilities loom so large they seem almost impossible to tackle. The only answer is just to begin.

Very young children seem to know the helpful powers of responsibility almost instinctively. They start out pleading: "Ask me to do it. Teach me to do it." Most of it centers on household tasks such as setting the table or feeding the dog or bringing in the newspapers. Children have the urge to be responsible.

As children grow older, they seem to lose some of this urge, at least at home. They begin to ask: "Do I really have to do that? Can't you get someone else? Later, okay?" They are testing us. Do we mean it? They are telling us that they have other things on their mind besides what we tell them to do. We know that it's part of growing up.

Teaching children to take care of themselves (brush teeth, make beds, pick up toys) is challenging, but tougher responsibilities are out there. Teaching children about truth and honesty is harder to teach than picking up clothes from the floor. We can tell if the floor is picked up, but we can't always tell if the child is telling the truth. We have to "grow" a responsible child. It starts small, even with household chores.

Look for Responsibility-Building Activities in this book to answer this question for the years ahead: How can I help my child do what's right...even and especially when I am not around?

• *About the MegaSkill Initiative: Moving into Action*

When we talk about Confidence and Motivation (two MegaSkills closely related to Initiative), we talk about "having" them. When we talk about Initiative, we talk about "taking" it. Initiative is what we do. It's action, based on our feelings of confidence, motivation, and hopefully common sense.

Most of the time we can go along without having to take very much initiative. Our lives are routine. We know what to expect most days. It's when change comes into our lives that we have to call on our initiative. For example, it's needed when, as adults, we start a new job or move to a different city.

We have to use initiative to make new friends, to get comfortable in new jobs. When traveling, it helps to have a map. That's what it is like when we work toward a goal. We need to keep on the road but also be able to see the interesting sights along the way. We need to be as organized as possible and set basic rules. Everything may not go exactly as we have planned, but there is a comfort in having a plan and having a sense of what might happen.

Look for Initiative-Building Activities in this book to answer this question for the years ahead: How can I help my child feel brave and have the get-up-and-go that it takes to get things moving?

• About the MegaSkill Perseverance: Completing What You Start

Perseverance is probably the foremost factor in a child's school success. It's mighty important all through life, but it's the key for doing well in school. We can have all the MegaSkills, but unless we have perseverance, success in school and on the job will be hard to come by.

When we see things begin to work because of our perseverance, we gain more confidence. It takes confidence and motivation to get started, but it takes perseverance to sustain the effort. Scientists, sports stars, literary figures, and artists all start with confidence. They have motivation, but they also all attest to how much they had to persevere.

Kids would be wise not to dream of being an overnight success. Nobel Prize winners wait decades for their awards. Sports figures practice and practice...and maybe then have a chance at the major league. Musicians work and work before they get to Carnegie Hall. There are very few overnight sensations.

Can we teach our children to persevere? Yes, but it is hard. Concentration spans are shorter now. Adults and children increasingly listen and think in sound bites. Teaching perseverance is more important than ever.

> *Look for Perseverance-Building Activities in this book to answer this question for the years ahead: How can I help my child keep at something, keep practicing and trying...especially when success doesn't come at first?*

• *About the MegaSkill Caring: Showing Concern for Others*

Most of us live, work, and care in the concentric circles of family, friends, school or job, and community. Concentric circles are circles with a common center, like those made when a stone is tossed into a pool. This causes new, ever-widening patterns.

Schools in general are not known as caring places. They're supposed to be hard, rigorous, academic—not soft and emotional. Yet it is in our daily lives, in school and on our jobs, where so many of our emotions are built and destroyed.

Caring matters because it provides the support we need to do well at home, in the classroom, and later on the job. Even large institutions, such as workplaces and schools, need to be warm places. They must nurture our abilities to do a good job.

When the going gets tough, we need to take a little time to say, "Let's think of at least two ways we can be nice to each other." It sounds corny, but it works. It's actually easier to think of two ways than it is to think of one. We need to look for opportunities to nurture our caring abilities.

Look for Caring-Building Activities in this book to answer this question for the years ahead: How can I help my child show love for the family and learn more about friendship?

• *About the MegaSkill Teamwork: Working with Others*

We are already members of a team. We are members of the family team, the class team, and the school team. Whether we like it or not, we are partners with a large number of people.

Job evaluations make it clear that to receive good "grades," employees are expected to work together to get the job done. On the football field, even the best player can't win the game alone. And an orchestra needs a stage full of cooperating players.

At school, even preschool, we are put into teams. Yet often we continue to be judged as individuals. That's one reason why teamwork that is supposed to make things easier may actually cause stress in the short run.

In the long run, teamwork enables us to learn more from one another. It helps build a sense of identity with the large group. It builds respect for diversity. The search is on for team players, not as "yes" people but as strong contributors, helping each other to be stronger.

Look for Teamwork-Building Activities in this book to answer this question for the years ahead: How can I help my child work more cooperatively with others and with me, too?

• *About the MegaSkill Common Sense: Using Good Judgment*

We need to know about cause and effect. We need to understand that what we say affects others. One way to build better judgment is by building our own common sense.

We need to show balance and judgment about handling time and money. We can learn to control our impulses in order to make more reasoned decisions.

We take chances every day, but we learn how to try to minimize our risks. For example, we may want to go ice skating. The ice on the lake looks thick and hard. But is it really?

How do we use our common sense? We use common sense to bring a pet inside in bad weather. We look both ways when crossing the street. We eat healthy foods, not junk food, for a healthy body. Even though we don't have common sense at first, we learn and relearn.

Look for Common Sense-Building Activities in this book to answer this question for the years ahead: How can I help my child know how to stay out of trouble and say "no" when "no" is the right answer?

• About the MegaSkill Problem Solving: Putting What You Know and What You Can Do into Action

No matter how old we are, we are always solving problems. Problems are the stuff of life. To be sure, there are certain problems we think of as strictly grown-up issues. But children are not spared, especially these days, from being involved in lots of what used to be adult-only activities. We have to find ways to help children know how to tackle problems.

Working on problems that lend themselves to solutions offers us a sense of real, personal achievement. It's the surge of satisfaction when we can figure out a short-cut to get downtown, find a new recipe the kids will eat or cook, discover a way to cut down on the monthly bills, or get the video camera to actually record.

We need a system inside our heads that enables us to face problems and try to manage them. That's our inner capacity for problem solving.

Ideas build on one another. They have a terrific ability to keep flowing as long as we keep drawing from the well.

Look for Problem Solving-Building Activities in this book to answer this question for the years ahead: How can I help my child learn how to identify a problem, think of a number of ways to solve it, and then try out some of these solutions?

• *About the MegaSkill Focus: Concentrating with a Goal in Mind*

For the very lucky few, focus is not a problem at all. Those are the folks we read about in the newspaper who know they want to swim across the English Channel or become a rocket scientist or a chess master. They just know. However, for most of us, focus is a continuing problem and a challenge.

That's why we must work on it from an early age. We can help children practice and build their ability to focus. Being able to focus for a longer period of time is a basic skill today.

Our lives have become more complicated. Life is coming at us fast. Focus has always been important. But it's always been assumed that we either have it or can be counted on to develop it. In slower times, that was probably the case.

Today, many of us feel caught in the whirlwind of so many choices and so much to do. The need for focus is not new—what's different is that "wasting our powers" is more dangerous today. The call for focus is being heard in schools and in the workplace as never before.

Look for Focus-Building Activities in this book to answer this question for the years ahead: How can I help my child acquire the habits of paying attention and concentrating on goals—when everything around us seems to be clamoring for attention all at once?

• *About the MegaSkill Respect: Showing Good Behavior, Courtesy, and Appreciation*

Teaching respect starts early. Unlike in earlier times, when it might have been assumed that respect was automatic, today it has to be taught—carefully taught.

For many generations, the traditional model for respect was authoritarian: "Children may be seen, but not heard." Times are different, and that's not bad. Overall, we live in a freer world that encourages us, even from the early years, to speak our minds and to follow our own dreams.

We need to be able to have give-and-take with our children, to teach them how to solve disagreements constructively by respecting the rights of others, including our own. We need to have reasonable expectations for our children, to explain them, to live by them, to enforce them, and to reward them as needed.

Children need to know how to follow rules and also how to ask questions. They need to be able to handle criticism and be fair to those who might disagree with them, including other children, parents, and teachers.

Look for Respect-Building Activities in this book to answer this question for the years ahead: What steps can I take to help my child develop meaningful respect, appreciation, and more?

25 Activities

4

*Starting Out:
Ages 1–2 Years*

"Play is often talked about as if it were a relief from serious learning. But for children, play is serious learning. Play is really the work of childhood."
—Fred Rogers, *Mr. Rogers' Neighborhood*

ACTIVITY	DEVELOPMENTAL THEME
Mud and Water	Create and Imagine
	Personal Competency
Paper Bag Puppets	Listen, Speak, and Do
What Shape Is That?	Reach Out and Explore
Climbing Mountains at Home	Reach Out and Explore
Spotlight Sounds	Reach Out and Explore
Watch My Face	Connect with Others
Lots of Color	Create and Imagine
Time for Bed	Promote Good Daily Habits
My Own Store	Create and Imagine
Which Hand?	Reach Out and Explore
Pot and Pan Music	Create and Imagine
Follow Me	Listen, Speak, and Do
Where Are You?	Create and Imagine
Rain Joy	Create and Imagine
We Help Each Other	Listen, Speak, and Do
Fabric Up and Down	Reach Out and Explore
We Do It Together	Connect with Others
Eyes, Ears, and Hands Tell Us	Listen, Speak, and Do
Tall and Short, Big and Small	Think and Organize
Up and Up	Create and Imagine
Where's the Ball?	Think and Organize

• *Welcome to Starting Out*

Oh, what a wondrous time this is!

Your child is into everything and you have to be watchful—careful but not fearful—when creating safe environments.

Make sure your house is ready for your young explorer. Have books that can be reached, vases that can't be reached, toys that are sturdy, pots and pans to make noise, and foods that build more muscle than fat.

Read stories over and over, use lots of words, and say the names of all the things in the room. You are building your child's love and use of language.

Use movement and put on music. Dance around the room with your child in your arms. Sing all the songs you know. Keep talking. Your child hears your words and makes responses.

Making a mess with finger paints and playing with water are great delights. Plan ahead with drop cloths on the floor and float toys in the bathtub.

Throw kisses, say bye-byes. Try the activities you find in this chapter. They are all about Learning and Loving!

1 CONFIDENCE: Mud and Water
Getting dirty for fun and learning

• *Developmental Theme: Create and Imagine*

All you need is water and dirt. A sunny day helps but is not necessary. For kids, nothing beats playing in the mud.

Bring out a pail and a little shovel or spoon and you have the tools for your child to create a mud masterpiece. You might want to add a toy truck for picking up and moving the mud. Talk about what you're creating as you're going along. Make sure your child is wearing old clothes that can get dirty.

Parents wearing old clothes can get right down into the mud too. Both of you can delight in building a mound or two and creating mud puddles in which to throw little pebbles and twigs.

Be prepared in advance for washing off dirt and ask your child to help clean up.

Note: It's nice to have a beach for this activity, but it can work as well in your own yard or in a nearby park.

2 CONFIDENCE: Paper Bag Puppets
Getting practice talking

• *Developmental Theme: Personal Competency*

Puppets can say a lot that children on their own might not say. And anybody, anytime, can make a puppet or two at home, easily and with no expense.

Save a few large paper bags. Carefully turn them inside out. Decorate the bags with big faces, using magic markers for eyes, nose, mouth, hair. Place these puppets on your hands and start talking.

You can use made-up people and made-up voices. It's great fun and a great vocabulary builder.

Note: Masks also work wonders for children, who lose their shyness and move into the world of make believe.

3 CONFIDENCE: What Shape Is That?

• *Developmental Theme: Listen, Speak, and Do*

WHY DO IT

This activity helps children identify basic shapes: circles, squares, and numbers.

MATERIALS

Grocery bags
Crayons or markers

HOW TO DO IT

Spread out the grocery bag. Draw a big circle on it. Ask your child to draw a smaller circle on another grocery bag. Talk about which circle is bigger and which is smaller.

Draw a big square on your bag. Draw a smaller square. Talk about other things in the room that are in the shape of circles or squares, such as plates, glasses, boxes.

ANOTHER IDEA

Use crackers shaped as circles, squares, or triangles. Let your child spread peanut butter and jam on them. Play a matching game with the shapes to make sandwiches.

 Children recognize basic shapes first and then move on to the more complex shapes, alphabet, and numbers. All of these are shapes, and this knowledge starts early.

4 MOTIVATION: *Climbing Mountains at Home*
Helping children practice crawl, jump, balance

• *Developmental Theme: Reach Out and Explore*

Whether children crawl or walk, they all need to move and test their bodies. We see this on playgrounds. It can happen at home too, without the slides. Just use pillows instead.

With your child helping you, find pillows you can place on the floor. Pile them high in some places, and pile them low in others. Together, you have created your child's own mountain climbing course at home.

Children love the rough and tumble of this safe challenge. When they fall down, they don't get hurt, and they get up again. It's great fun, and soon they call to you from the highest mountain: "Look, I am at the top!"

5 MOTIVATION: *Spotlight Sounds*
Helping children build vocabulary

• *Developmental Theme: Reach Out and Explore*

Build on the thrill little ones have of playing with a flashlight in a darkened room.

Sit in the dark and ask your child to point with a flashlight to different objects around the room. Ask your child to name each object. As the game progresses, your child will be able to name and remember more and more objects around the house.

EFFORT: Watch My Face
Helping young children concentrate and imitate

• *Developmental Theme: Connect with Others*

Young children spend a lot of time watching their parents' faces. Often they imitate what they see, especially when parents smile and laugh.

Take a few minutes for you and your child to make faces together. Ask your child to do what you do. Start with a big smile and laugh. Try a variety of faces and ask your child to imitate you: Close your eyes, open them wide, wink with one eye, and then the other.

Trade places and let your child make faces that you follow.

EFFORT: Lots of Color
Helping children take pride in their artwork

• *Developmental Theme: Create and Imagine*

Children love color. They love paint, and they need to express themselves. Putting brush to paper comes even before language.

You don't need fancy equipment: a few brushes, some large pieces of paper, and watercolor paints. Paint alongside your child. Dress yourself and your child in old clothes or smocks. Prepare for spills in advance by putting paper or a large cloth on the floor.

Share your paintings and talk about them. Post them for everyone to see and admire.

8 RESPONSIBILITY: Time for Bed
Helping children know what's expected

• Developmental Theme: Promote Good Daily Habits

Convincing some children to leave the excitement of family life and go to bed is not easy. It can help when children learn what's expected—especially the routines that lead up to going to bed. These include changing clothes, washing up, brushing teeth, and reading stories.

Draw pictures (or find them in magazines) showing pre-bedtime routines. Place them in order. Number them (one to four or more). Post these pictures for your child to see on the way to bed. Talk about them. In this way, your child will learn to follow the steps to bedtime.

9 RESPONSIBILITY: My Own Store
Helping children recognize foods

• Developmental Theme: Create and Imagine

Everyone likes to shop, even young children. They don't have to go to the store to do it.

Save empty cereal boxes and other clean food containers to have a make-believe supermarket at home. Keep the labels on and make sure the tops are closed tightly. Encourage your child to put the containers on tables and low shelves. Talk together about these different foods.

Before you both go to the real supermarket, your child can take out these food containers. They will be reminders of what you may need to buy.

10 *INITIATIVE: Which Hand?*
Making good guesses

• *Developmental Theme: Reach Out and Explore*

This is a game of hide-and-seek using a small object in your hands. Hide an object in one hand. Ask your child to guess which hand the object is in: right or left.

Place the object—a small stone or pebble—in the same hand for several tries. Let your child get comfortable with the correct answer before changing hands.

Then, provide a clue that the object may change hands. Thrust out both hands again and ask: "Which hand?" When your child guesses it correctly, say, "Now, we are going to keep changing hands. Watch carefully."

Try different patterns: one left, one right, two left, one right, etc. Keep the interest high. When your child is ready, trade places and let your child play "Which Hand?" with you.

11 *INITIATIVE: Pot and Pan Music*
Helping children make rhythmic noise

• *Developmental Theme: Create and Imagine*

Children like to make noise. You have the right noise makers in your own kitchen cupboard: pots, pans, forks, and spoons. Bring them out. Lay them on a clean place on the floor, and sit down with your child to play music.

You or your child can lead off with a few beats. Then repeat the same number of beats. Try to create patterns and rhythms in the noise, using different numbers of beats that are loud and soft. This provides practice in making noise that pleases the ear and builds listening skills.

12 PERSEVERANCE: Follow Me
Helping children pay careful attention

• *Developmental Theme: Listen, Speak, and Do*

Very young children are great imitators. Ask your child to listen and watch you very carefully, and then imitate what you do. Start with big gestures and put words to what you are doing. Point to the parts of the body you will be moving. Say:

I am closing my eyes. Now close yours.

I am raising my right arm. Now raise yours.

I am raising my left arm. Now raise yours.

Move your legs, right and left. Wiggle your nose. Shake your head. Depending on your child's walking ability, turn backwards, walk slower and then faster. Your child follows you—the leader! Then, trade places.

13 PERSEVERANCE: Where Are You?
Learning where activities happen

• *Developmental Theme: Create and Imagine*

Indoors and out, children and parents rush about at play, at home, at school, and at jobs. Find magazine pictures to illustrate these activities.

Ask your child to look for pictures of people doing different activities. Which ones are done indoors and which are done outdoors? Examples: Vacuuming is done indoors. Running is done outdoors.

With your help as needed, ask your child to find and cut out pictures of people doing activities your family likes to do indoors and outdoors. Talk together about what you see.

Mix up the pictures. Ask your child to put the pictures of outdoor activities in one pile and the pictures of indoor activities in another pile. Together use the pictures to tell a story. "This is how we help each other. This is what we do inside the house. This is what we do outdoors."

14 *CARING: Rain Joy*
Helping children take delight in nature

• *Developmental Theme: Create and Imagine*

On a warm, rainy day, surprise children by dressing them in bathing suits and taking them outside to enjoy a gentle summer shower.

Together, dance around and catch raindrops in your hands or your mouth.

Put on boots and jump in the puddles. Talk to your child about how you jumped in the rain when you were young. Look at how water collects in cracks and pot-holes. Move the water about and create a river. Water delights us all, no matter how old we are.

15 *CARING: We Help Each Other*
Helping children listen and do

• *Developmental Theme: Listen, Speak, and Do*

Think of a real job that your young child can do, along with two or three instructions for this task. Ask your child to listen carefully as you say these instructions.

For example: 1. Bring the waste paper basket to the kitchen. 2. Help put its contents into the big kitchen can. 3. Take the empty basket back. 4. Let me know when you are finished.

Then, trade places. Ask your child to give you some instructions to follow.

16 TEAMWORK: *Fabric Up and Down*
Helping children follow and create movement

• *Developmental Theme: Reach Out and Explore*

This activity is played with a long stretch of fabric, the lighter the better.

You and your child are a team. Each of you holds tight to an end of the fabric and moves it all about, up and down, all around. This activity is most fun outdoors on a beautiful and windy day when the wind catches the fabric and moves it about. Watch and talk about how the wind moves the cloth.

Try moving the fabric in different ways: jump up as high as you can, then crouch down bringing it low to the ground. Think of as many different ways as possible to move the material about.

After awhile, let children take the lead and you follow their movements and directions.

17 TEAMWORK: *We Do It Together*
Helping children work with us

• *Developmental Theme: Connect with Others*

Even very young children can work with parents or caregivers, as members of a team.

They can share our food: You take a bite. Your child takes a bite.

They can ring bells with us: You ring a bell. Your child rings a bell and then you ring together.

They can crumple paper with us: You crumple paper. Your child follows and then you do it together.

You blow a whistle or play a drum. Your child follows. With two whistles and a drum, you have an orchestra.

18 COMMON SENSE: *Eyes, Ears, and Hands Tell Us*
Helping children observe and name objects

• *Developmental Theme: Listen, Speak, and Do*

We put words to what we see, hear, and touch: different colors, loud noise or soft noise, rough or smooth, etc. Look around the room with your child and name:
  • The biggest thing in the room and the smallest
  • The noises you hear: the cars outside, the hum of the air conditioner or TV

Look around outside and name:
  • The colors of the cars
  • The music of the birds
  • The biggest and smallest things

19 COMMON SENSE: *Tall and Short, Big and Small*
Helping children observe and respond

• *Developmental Theme: Think and Organize*

Point out sizes of things around the house. Show children objects in the room that are big, small, tall, and short. Who is taller? Mother or child? Which lamp is smaller? Do you want a smaller helping or a bigger helping of food? Who has bigger feet? Smaller hands? Questions and answers bounce off each other. Soon it is a game that your child will start playing with you.

Keep track of your child's growth. As soon as your child can stand upright, mark her height (with the date) at the edge of a door. Every six months, record your growing child.

20 PROBLEM SOLVING: Up and Up

- *Developmental Theme: Create and Imagine*

WHY DO IT

This activity helps children develop hand-eye coordination and results in a really tall tower.

MATERIALS

Several clean, empty cans with tops carefully removed. Use empty soup cans, tuna cans, soda cans, or any cans that are not heavy.

Small boxes can also be used in place of cans.

HOW TO DO IT

Place all the cans in front of your child. Build a small tower yourself with three of the cans. Say, "Look, here's a tower." Your child will be delighted with your success.

Now it's your child's turn. Ask him to stack as many items as possible—up and up. Some may fall, and that's okay. Try, try again.

ANOTHER IDEA

Try making your towers next to each other. Have a little contest. Children love to win. Some cans will fall over because they need to fit and be the right size. Keep trying.

 Children love to build. We see this when children build with blocks. Cans and boxes are inexpensive alternatives that provide a variety of building experiences.

21 PROBLEM SOLVING: Where's the Ball?

• *Developmental Theme: Think and Organize*

WHY DO IT
This activity helps children use their eyes and ears. They watch for and locate the spot where the ball rolls.

MATERIALS
A big ball

HOW TO DO IT
Start this game with you and your child on the floor. Roll the ball to your child, who then rolls it back to you.

   After a few back-and-forths, roll the ball to a nearby corner of the room or other hiding place. Ask "Where is the ball? Look all around." Your child finds the ball, brings it back, and you roll it away again. Your child finds it again.

ANOTHER IDEA
Trade places. Let your child roll the ball away from you and ask, "Where is the ball?"

Keep this game going until you have exhausted every hiding place in the room. It's an easy exercise that introduces basic elements of problem solving.

22 FOCUS: Bathroom Writing
Writing with broad strokes on mirrors

• *Developmental Theme: Reach Out and Explore*

Mirror, mirror, on the wall, who is the "writingest" one of all? Answer: the child who makes bold-stroke As and Bs and all kinds of letter shapes on steamed-up mirrors.

These shapes, written big and brashly, are part of the development of "gross motor" muscles, which are needed later for the small muscle control used in handwriting.

Shapes are everywhere in the bathroom—oval soaps, rectangular sponges, cylinders galore, glasses with their circular bottoms. Shapes are also what make up the alphabet. Point to the different shapes in the bathroom, name them, examine them, and let your child draw them on the mirror.

23 FOCUS: Say What I Say
Helping children listen and make joyful noises

• *Developmental Theme: Connect with Others*

From infancy on, children are great babblers. When talking with your child, you repeat and imitate these sounds. This is the language of bonding.

Ask your child to listen to you make sounds. Let her repeat the sounds you are making. Make these sounds easy to remember and repeat: single syllables like "oh," "my," and "hi." They can be sounds of the alphabet, numbers, nonsense words, anything you make up. They don't have to be repeated exactly.

Use the same activity with music, singing words from favorite songs and asking your child to sing along with you.

24 *RESPECT: You Draw Me, I Draw You*
Paying attention to others

• *Developmental Theme: Personal Competency*

Children are almost never too young to learn that there are other people in the world. This activity stays close to home. You and your child will be drawing face pictures of each other.

You may want to start first. Say, "Here is how I see you: here are your eyes, your nose, your mouth, your hair, your ears" and draw your child's face.

Now your child (with or without your help) gets the chance to draw your face: "Here is how I see you: your eyes, your nose, your mouth" and so on.

Talk about what you see in each other's faces. Put the drawings side by side. Do we look happy? How do we look? Most of all, we care about and love each other.

25 RESPECT: Keeping Things Nice

• *Developmental Theme: Promote Good Daily Habits*

WHY DO IT

Children may receive many (perhaps too many) nice toys. Often these don't get taken care of. Even very young children can learn to "respect" their toys and clothes.

MATERIALS

Toys that need good treatment

HOW TO DO IT

Sit your child down with some toys in a cozy place on the floor. Teach your child how to handle a delicate doll or truck. Demonstrate by showing how you pick objects up and put them down, without throwing them about.

Trade places. Ask your child to show you how to handle toys gently.

ANOTHER IDEA

Make sure that your child has a place to keep his toys, a reachable shelf that makes it easier to put toys away carefully.

Children can be rough on toys and clothes. Of course, some will break and tear. Yet, sometimes we parents forget to show our young ones how to take care of things so that they will last longer and provide longer pleasure.

29 Activities

5

Keeping Going:
Ages 2–3 Years

"Adam and Eve had many
advantages but the prin-
cipal one was that they
escaped teething."
—Mark Twain

ACTIVITY   DEVELOPMENTAL THEME

Same or Different . . . . Listen, Speak, and Do
Mystery Box . . . . Pre-Read and Respond

Let's Pretend . . . . Create and Imagine
Stop and Go Walk . . . . Reach Out and Explore

Disappearing Letters . . . . Reach Out and Explore
Who's Talking Now? . . . . Connect with Others
Sense and Say . . . . Pre-Read and Respond
Count Down and Up . . . . Think and Organize

Which One? . . . . Think and Organize
Slow and Fast Walk at Home . . . . . Personal Competency
Music all Around Us . . . . Create and Imagine

Picture Reading . . . . Pre-Read and Respond
Little Creatures . . . . Reach Out and Explore
Mix and Match . . . . Reach Out and Explore

Say Something Nice . . . . Connect with Others
Is It Your Birthday? . . . . Create and Imagine

How Do I Feel? . . . . Connect with Others
Our Grocery Words . . . . Listen, Speak, and Do
Fingertip Words . . . . Listen, Speak, and Do

Fitness Starts Early . . . . Promote Good Daily Habits
Listen and Learn . . . . Promote Good Daily Habits

• *Welcome to Keeping Going*

Your child is now walking, even running. She is building towers, climbing steps, saying new words, and starting sentences. This is a challenging and remarkable period. Skills and abilities are emerging. Talk, talk, talk together. Language is more than a game. It is the magic that builds later school and work success.

Play lots of pretend games with dolls, puppets, and trucks. Tell stories to each other. Read, read, read, even if your child asks to read the same book over and over. Keep a corner for art supplies. Find easy ways to contain the mess. Join with your child in creating drawings and block towers. Let children help you break through to your own creative impulses.

Reach out to find other children nearby whose parents may want to join in a play group. Both you and your child need to be with peers. Your child is not the only one who needs support. During naptime, take a break and a rest.

Try the activities in this chapter. They are truly about Learning and Loving.

1 *CONFIDENCE: Same or Different*

• *Developmental Theme: Listen, Speak, and Do*

WHY DO IT

This activity helps children notice when things are alike or different. This is an important early thinking skill.

MATERIALS

Laundry to be sorted

HOW TO DO IT

Demonstrate how to match two laundry items such as two small towels. Then ask your child to match other laundry items: handkerchiefs, underwear, socks. Your child can match laundry items by color and make a separate laundry pile for each member of the family.

ANOTHER IDEA

Place objects on a table, such as two forks and a spoon or table knife; two plates and a cup; or two sticks and a rock. Talk about which things are alike and which are different. Ask your child to pick the item that is different.

 Children are young scientists, trying to figure out what's happening. They organize in their own minds the ways of the world around them. Parents can help by giving children these organizing experiences.

2 *CONFIDENCE: Mystery Box*
Helping children build vocabulary

• *Developmental Theme: Pre-Read and Respond*

Prepare a box containing small objects such as a key, sponge, scrap piece of material, scouring pad, and so on. This is a "mystery box" of textures. Have your child close his eyes, reach in, pick an object, and describe its texture. Let him guess the object. If there is time, trade places with your child.

Let your child find and name three things that are soft, three that are hard, three that are smooth, and three that are rough. Go on to include as many textures as you both can name.

3 CONFIDENCE: Let's Pretend

• *Developmental Theme: Create and Imagine*

WHY DO IT

Children love and need to pretend. They explore and test what it's like to be a cowboy, a prince, or a princess. This kind of play expands a child's world.

MATERIALS

A costume box filled with different kinds of old clothes
Radio or music player
Imagination

HOW TO DO IT

Fill a box with clothes your child can use to become new characters. Hats, scarves, and masks are especially useful. Announce that the play is almost ready to begin: "Get dressed and I'll put on the music."

Your child gets into her costume, picking what she wants from the costume box. Now comes the big moment: the lights go dim, the music begins, and your child dances about as the character she has become.

Ask: "Who are you? I would never have guessed!"

ANOTHER IDEA

Trade places. Parents dress up using the costume box materials and dance about while children make the music.

Use a variety of ways to build your child's confidence; music and poetry are great stimulators. Ask your child to tell you how music makes her feel. Sing and dance every chance you get.

4 *MOTIVATION: Stop and Go Walk*

• *Developmental Theme: Reach Out and Explore*

WHY DO IT

Children are learning all the time. This pleasurable learning activity is a nature and reading walk, using the objects and signs in your neighborhood.

MATERIALS

Objects from nature, such as sticks and stones
Signs already in place in your neighborhood

HOW TO DO IT

Before going on the walk, talk about signs you might see. Talk about their shapes and colors. Look for a stop sign. Try to find another stop sign.

While on the walk, ask your child to pick up nature objects that he would like to have in his collection. Caution children to avoid extremely dirty, sharp, and unsanitary objects.

Back at home, provide a special shelf or box for the collection of nature objects found on the walk. With your child, group these objects together to see how they are the same or different.

ANOTHER IDEA

Make up a question that has a choice of two answers: one answer is a word from a sign in the neighborhood; the other is a word that sounds similar. For example, "Do you cross the street when the sign says *walk* or *talk?*"

 Children may want to give some found objects as "thinking of you" gifts to friends and relatives.

5 MOTIVATION: Disappearing Letters

• *Developmental Theme: Reach Out and Explore*

WHY DO IT

This activity develops hand-eye coordination and provides practice in writing big letters and numbers.

MATERIALS

Bucket
Water
Paintbrushes

HOW TO DO IT

Fill a large bucket with water. Go to a walkway, driveway, concrete or blacktop area outdoors. Along with your child, write letters, names, and words using the paintbrush and water. The writing will "magically" disappear as it dries.

Say these letters and words aloud to your child. Talk about the words and drawings you both paint.

Then write more. Mistakes also vanish.

ANOTHER IDEA

Paint your words in a sunny place and also in a shady place. Check to see which words dry faster.

 This activity expands motor skills and language abilities.

6 *EFFORT: Who's Talking Now?*

• *Developmental Theme: Connect with Others*

WHY DO IT

This activity gets children listening closely to voices: their own, and those of parents, friends, and relatives.

MATERIALS

Your child's voice and the voices around her

HOW TO DO IT

Announce to your child that in one minute there will be a "special listening time." Say, "Be sure that your ears are ready. You will close your eyes and listen very hard to tell who is talking."

Your child sits quietly and waits for a voice. If you are the only person at home, disguise your voice and say several words, such as "bow, wow, wow." Then ask your child, "Who's talking?" See if your child can recognize you.

Raise and lower your voice and see if your child still recognizes you, no matter how your voice sounds.

Now let your child test you—encourage her to disguise her voice. Listen carefully, but be ready to make a mistake or two and say that your child's voice is someone else. This makes the game more fun.

ANOTHER IDEA

Involve two friends, neighbors, or relatives. Ask your child to listen to these voices and tell *who is talking now*. When your child recognizes every voice spoken normally, then disguise voices and the game continues.

 Children first learn to communicate by listening. Telling stories develops listening skills and builds vocabulary for later reading and writing.

7 *EFFORT: Sense and Say*

• *Developmental Theme: Pre-Read and Respond*

WHY DO IT
Asking and answering questions extends a child's use of language.

MATERIALS
Three small boxes and an assortment of items that can be touched, smelled, or tasted (see below).

HOW TO DO IT
Place the following items into three boxes.
- Touch box: cotton, a stone, a piece of sandpaper
- Smell box: an assortment of ingredients from the kitchen, such as mustard, cinnamon, vinegar
- Taste box: salt, pepper, and a piece of candy

Smell the mustard together. Ask your child what it reminds him of. He may recall a picnic on the beach where sea gulls landed and waves pounded hard on shore. Explore the other items in the boxes and ask similar questions. This activity will prompt your child to talk more descriptively.

ANOTHER IDEA
Similar smells and senses offer consistency of experience. Keep identifying the senses you and your child recognize.

 Remember that children need routines. When is bedtime? When are mealtimes? What times are set for TV watching and computer use? The more regular those routines are, the better. Routines help children learn what to expect of the world around them, of others, and of themselves.

8 RESPONSIBILITY: Count Down and Up

Getting acquainted with numbers around the home

• Developmental Theme: Think and Organize

Children start to count numbers very early. It can be an abstract concept until they put the numbers concretely to what they know and experience. Try the following counting activities to help your child get acquainted with numbers.

Name and count the number of people who live in your house.

Ask your child to count his fingers and then to count yours. Are they the same number? Do the same with toes.

Count the number of chairs around the kitchen table. Count the number of lamps in the living room.

Count and count and count! The world, even our own home, is filled with numbers.

9 RESPONSIBILITY: Which One?

Helping children make choices

• Developmental Theme: Think and Organize

Children can learn to take responsibility early if you offer them clear choices. These have to be choices that parents can live with, and they need to be very limited—two or three at the most. Give your child the following choices:

- Which shirt do you want to wear today?
- What song should we sing?
- What book should we read?
- Where should we go on our walk?
- What soup do we want for lunch?

To make it more challenging, ask for your child's suggestions for choices you should make, too.

10 *INITIATIVE: Slow and Fast Walk at Home*
Getting in touch with our daily world

• *Developmental Theme: Personal Competency*

Walk through each room of the house.

Name, as fast as you can, at least five different things you and your child see in each room, from lamp to rug to telephone and so on. Look for what's made out of wood, or of cloth, or of glass. Walk up to these items. Touch them. Talk about how they feel.

Look for small things, such as a doorstop. Look for big things, such as a sofa.

Ask your child to find an object that you name, such as a spoon, pan, or plate, and show or bring it to you.

11 INITIATIVE: Music All Around Us

• *Developmental Theme: Create and Imagine*

WHY DO IT

It is said that music soothes the savage soul. Actually, it does more than that. It soothes and delights children, especially melodic classic, folk, and nursery songs.

MATERIALS

CD player, radio, or other music playing device

HOW TO DO IT

Start a small collection of your child's favorite music. Talk about and name these CDs.

When you read stories together, ask your child to pick music to listen to as you read. Encourage background selections.

Put your child's name to music. Rather than "Old McDonald had a farm," try "Little Susie has a farm." Pick any song that has easy lyrics, and you can substitute your child's name.

ANOTHER IDEA

Use music as background throughout the day: play it while giving your child a bath (think water music), or while preparing food and eating (think soft, soothing music).

 Music has been discussed as a force for building brain power. While that is still a controversial topic, what is clear is that music can help soothe everyone's hectic days. Favorite music can also be a force for bonding between parent and child.

12 PERSEVERANCE: Picture Reading

• *Developmental Theme: Pre-Read and Respond*

WHY DO IT

Long before your child can read, you introduce the wonderful world of books to your child when you look at pictures.

MATERIALS

Two or three short picture books
Magazines with pictures

HOW TO DO IT

With your child next to you or on your lap, open a book. Before reading the story, go through the pages pointing out the pictures. It might be a book about animals, for example. Name the animals you both see. After you name what's in the pictures, your child repeats what you say.

Children often want to hear the same stories over and over. So be sure to pick books you like too. Read the story slowly and with feeling. Try to use different voices for each character. The love of reading starts here!

ANOTHER IDEA

Cut out magazine pictures similar to those in the books. Post or paste them in a scrapbook. Your child can play with these pictures and start naming them on his own.

 Give your child time to concentrate on pictures in books, and to take a close look at stones and flowers as you take walks. Often we hurry children along because we are in a rush. Make a special point to give children some unhurried time, to take a long look, to start to build their capacity to persevere.

13 PERSEVERANCE: Little Creatures

• *Developmental Theme: Reach Out and Explore*

WHY DO IT

Finding a little bug or worm and taking care of it is a lesson in nature and perseverance.

MATERIALS

Small creature such as a worm or garden bug
Small jar or cup with airholes in the top
Damp grass for food inside the jar

HOW TO DO IT

Walk with your child in the backyard or a nearby park. Look for a little worm or bug to take home in your special jar. Look beneath rocks and dig through top soil and you are sure to find a little creature or two.

With your child, look carefully at the creature. How does it move? If you can feel it, talk about what it feels like.

After one day in the jar, check how the little creature is doing. Now release it back into its home in the yard.

ANOTHER IDEA

Get books from the library about worms, bugs, and other small creatures. Small children enjoy hearing about even smaller bodies.

 Encourage interest in nature and what is going on outside, in all seasons. Look at the birds and what they eat. If you can, set up a bird feeder so that your child can sit by the window and see what's happening in all kinds of weather.

14 *PERSEVERANCE: Mix and Match*
Helping children identify alike and different

• *Developmental Theme: Reach Out and Explore*

Gather a group of containers with lids, such as jars, freezer containers, and plastic bowls. Take off the lids and mix them up. Ask your child to place the lids on the matching containers.

Now find objects or pictures that are exactly alike: two forks, a handful of pennies, three yellow crayons, etc. Mix them up. Ask your child to group together the ones that are the same.

These are steps on the road to logical thinking.

15 CARING: Say Something Nice

• *Developmental Theme: Connect with Others*

WHY DO IT

This activity gives children practice being nice.

HOW TO DO IT

Make it a family activity to end each day by saying something nice about each other.

Praise needs to be as specific as possible. General praise such as "You are wonderful!" tends to be overlooked. What everyone needs and appreciates is specific praise. You might say to your child, "I like the way you helped your brother find his lost shoe" or "I noticed that you got ready for bed the first time I asked."

ANOTHER IDEA

Trade places. Parents can write a child's dictated message. Your child might say, "I liked the cookie. Thank you."

 Whether spoken or written, these messages help children express their positive feelings and learn how good it feels to receive nice words.

16 CARING: Is It Your Birthday?
Using the calendar to keep track of time

• Developmental Theme: Create and Imagine

Children generally have their own birthday celebrations. Let's help them show their caring by involving them in celebrations for mom, dad, brothers, sisters, and the extended family.

Use a calendar with big squares for days. Start with the date of your child's birthday. Say the month and day aloud and ask your child to mark the square. Now find the birthday dates on the calendar for others in your family. Say these dates aloud, point to the squares on the calendar, and let your child mark them.

Talk about these as the months fly by. "Is your birthday in this month? Is mine? Whose birthday is it?" Now ask, "What should we do to celebrate?" How about making a card—a few colored scribbles will be fine. Or pick some wild flowers or decorate a placemat. Keep it easy to do. The goal is to remember others and to create memories.

17 CARING: How Do I Feel?
Helping children understand feelings.

• Developmental Theme: Connect with Others

When children identify their own feelings, they also learn about how others feel. Here's how to help children share their feelings. Make an "About Me" book.

Staple together four pieces of paper. Make one "little book" for yourself and one for your child.

Ask your child the following questions, and write the answers in his book. Add questions of your own, too.

I am happy when: _____

I am sad when: _____

I think it's funny when: _____

At home I like to: _____

Prompt your child with answers you give for your own book. There are no "right" answers.

18 TEAMWORK: Our Grocery Words

• *Developmental Theme: Listen, Speak, and Do*

WHY DO IT
This activity helps your child match words with everyday grocery foods.

MATERIALS
Bag of grocery foods

HOW TO DO IT
Tell your child that together you are going to put the groceries away using words. Describe an item in the bag, such as "a can with red on it," or "a big box of soap." Then ask your child to bring the item to you after listening to your description. Ask her to group together the items that look alike and name the items. "You have two cans of soup."

ANOTHER IDEA
At mealtime, talk about the foods that each person is eating. Talk about who likes the different foods and why.

 Be talkative with your child. Research tells us that the size of children's vocabulary depends largely on how much parents and caregivers talk to them. It's the connection between these words and real experiences that enables children to hold on to and use these words.

19 TEAMWORK: Fingertip Words

• *Developmental Theme: Listen, Speak, and Do*

WHY DO IT
This activity helps children build vocabulary.

MATERIALS
Common household objects

HOW TO DO IT
Talk with your child about how different objects feel when touched. Explain texture words, such as "soft," "hard," "rough," and "smooth."

Ask your child to touch a soft object such as a pillow, a cat, or a fluffy rug. Talk about "soft."

Find other objects for your child to touch as you talk about the meanings of "hard" (floor), "rough" (sandpaper), "smooth" (mirror), and so on.

ANOTHER IDEA
Prepare a "mystery box" of textures containing small objects such as a key, sponge, scrap piece of material, scouring pad, and so on. Have your child close his eyes, reach in, pick an object, and describe its texture. See if he can guess the object. If there is time, trade places.

 Let your child find and name one thing that is soft, one that is hard, one that is smooth. Go on to as many textures as you both can name.

20 TEAMWORK: Fitness Starts Early

• *Developmental Theme: Promote Good Daily Habits*

WHY DO IT

This activity introduces your child to number skills, and it gives you both exercise.

MATERIALS

Ball (any large, round ball that bounces)
TV, radio, CD player (or any other music playing device)

HOW TO DO IT

Think of this as an easy exercise plan for a few days. Each day you will do more exercise.

Choose a place indoors that's safe for jumping and playing with bouncing balls (when the weather is good, choose a place outside). Turn on some music. Stand or sit, and roll the ball to each other at least five times. Then step or jump in place at least five times. Count to be sure that each of you does your part. This will help introduce your child to number skills.

ANOTHER IDEA

Have a contest. Get all members of the family to take turns rolling the ball and jumping.

 Keep track of each person's exercise totals each day. For example, Grace jumped five times on Day One. How many times did Mom jump on Day Two? Try to keep a record.

21 COMMON SENSE: *Listen and Learn*

• *Developmental Theme: Promote Good Daily Habits*

WHY DO IT
This activity helps build observation and listening skills.

MATERIALS
Kitchen utensils
Magazines with pictures of people

HOW TO DO IT
As your child watches, make sounds with several objects: spoons and forks, dishes and pans. Ask your child to listen to the sounds and then close his eyes. Then make the same sounds again, one at a time. Ask your child to tell you what utensils are making these sounds.

Now let your child make sounds for you to name.

ANOTHER IDEA
Look through magazines with your child to find pictures of people making sounds such as singing, playing instruments, or driving cars. Talk about sounds we hear every day.

Parents, remember to talk about safety reminders for some sounds. When dealing with kitchen utensils, avoid sharp objects such as knives and explain to your child how to handle utensils, such as forks, carefully.

22 COMMON SENSE: Where Did It Go?
Helping children follow the action

• *Developmental Theme: Think and Organize*

Here's a version of peekaboo that takes children to the next level.

Place three items on a table and let your child know that one of them will be taken away. Ask your child to close her eyes while you take one item away. Close the gap where the object was removed.

Now the big question is: What is gone and where did it go? Children love this guessing game and it's more than fun. It demands focus and further guessing about where the object might be now.

23 PROBLEM SOLVING: What Happens When?
Helping children make discoveries

• *Developmental Theme: Reach Out and Explore*

On a hot summer day, invite your child outside with you to cool off. Turn on the water from a hose or faucet and try some easy experiments. What happens when you put your thumb over the hole? How high can you make the water go? What does the water feel like on your toes?

Watch your child make discoveries. Water squirts, splashes, and falls from different heights. Talk about what you see.

24 PROBLEM SOLVING: Our World Around Us

• *Developmental Theme: Reach Out and Explore*

WHY DO IT

This activity builds your child's environmental awareness at a young age. You can do it in your backyard or a nearby park.

MATERIALS

Coat hanger
Small bottle
Magnifying glass
Cardboard paper towel roll.

HOW TO DO IT

With your child, focus your vision on the ground below. Place the coat hanger on the ground. Look at the area of ground that falls inside the coat hanger. Examine carefully what you both find inside its edges.

Put a bug in a clear pill bottle. Look closely at all its parts and watch its activity for a few minutes. Then let it out of the bottle.

Look through the cardboard tube. This helps you to focus on a single object or area.

ANOTHER IDEA

Take a "picture" with your eyes. Look at a scene and try to remember everything about it. Look at a stone, a leaf, or a bird. Try to remember it. Use a magnifying glass to see more details.

"Look hard" activities make us more aware of things we might walk by without noticing. Use these activities to heighten awareness. They help us get more out of life!

25 *FOCUS: Opposites Attract*
Learning about opposites/building vocabulary

• *Developmental Theme: Pre-Read and Respond*

Here's an opportunity for you and your child to have fun with words and concepts that are opposites. At the same time, you will be moving your bodies to illustrate these opposites.

- What's high? What's low? What's up and what's down? Raise your hands and lower them. Stand tall and sit down.
- What's near and what's far? Walk to a nearby spot in the room and then to a far one.
- What's hot and what's cold? Check this at your sink faucets (make sure to keep the hot water at a safe temperature).

Continue with opposites that are easily illustrated: fat and thin, left and right, long and short.

It's a game and a lot more including following directions, paying attention and building vocabulary.

26 *FOCUS: Word of the Day*
Helping children collect words, one by one

• *Developmental Theme: Pre-Read and Respond*

Have your child select a special word for the day. This can be a word your child already knows or wants to know. In a way, these are magic words, words full of personal meanings or lovely sounds.

Then write the word on a piece of paper or file card. Prewriters can dictate their special words and make drawings on the cards to illustrate the words.

Each day your child adds a new word. If you are using file cards, place them in a file or recipe box. Your child will love to look at and read the words.

27 FOCUS: Clap, Snap, Rap

• *Developmental Theme: Listen, Speak, and Do*

WHY DO IT

This activity helps your child practice settling down, making an effort, and concentrating on sounds.

HOW TO DO IT

Have your child close his eyes and listen carefully to the sounds that you will be making. Rap on the table, clap your hands, snap your fingers, yawn, cough, hum, and so on. Stop after each sound. Then name each sound you made.

Switch roles and ask your child to make sounds for you to name. Clap your hands in a rhythmic pattern. Ask your child to clap in the same pattern.

ANOTHER IDEA

Open a door or a window and ask your child to listen for sounds outside. Name the sounds your child hears. Add everyday sounds such as water running, a doorbell ringing, and a clock chiming.

 Focus can be hard to measure. What one person can complete with ease requires extra time and energy for another. Ask your child to tell you about his successes—getting to the top of the slide for the first time, tasting a new food, making a new friend. For some children these may be easy activities. For others they are accomplishments that take a lot of focus.

28 RESPECT: How Are Your Manners Today?

• *Developmental Theme: Connect with Others*

WHY DO IT

This activity gives young children practice using the words "please" and "thank you."

HOW TO DO IT

Talk about the words "please" and "thank you." Hold a pretend or real family dinner. Ask your child to "please" pass you the salt or anything else safe and handy. Say "thank you."

Now your child asks you to pass a cup or a fork "please." You say "thank you." Keep doing this so that your child feels comfortable using these words.

ANOTHER IDEA

Talk together about table manners: how we sit, how we try not to drop food, how we use napkins, how we chew our food, etc.

 Be a good role model. Make sure your child sees you using your good manners. Your child will learn to behave the way you do.

29 *RESPECT: That's Nice, That's Not*
Seeing good behavior in action

• *Developmental Theme: Personal Competency*

We often tell our kids to stop a certain rude behavior with words like, "That's not nice." But one good example can be worth many warning words. When you are waiting in a supermarket line, ask your child to look around at other children and tell you who is acting nice and who isn't.

It will be clear to your child that yelling, shouting, crying, and pushing are not signs of acting nice. Other children will be sitting or standing quietly, not making demands, helping their parents.

Real life examples are excellent teachers.

32 Activities

6

Sailing Along: Ages Advanced 2–3 Years

"Every child is an artist. The problem is how to remain an artist once we grow up."
— Pablo Picasso

Bye, Bye Fear . . . . Connect with Others
I'm Thinking! . . . . Think and Organize
"Time-Out" for Toys . . . . Listen, Speak, and Do
TV Time—Yes or No? . . . . Promote Good Daily Habits

Walk the Line . . . . Reach Out and Explore
In the Bag . . . . Listen, Speak, and Do
Watch Carefully . . . . Reach Out and Explore

Happy and Sad . . . . Personal Competency
Wait, Wait . . . . Personal Competency
Saying It So It Works . . . . Promote Good Daily Habits

• *Welcome to Sailing Along*

Your older toddler wants to tell you a lot. As playing and exploring with toys continues, now comes a lot more thinking.

At this age, your child becomes involved in figuring out things and doing activities along with you. These include doing household chores, bringing in the newspaper, helping put clothes away, sorting dark and light items for the wash, and putting away toys. Talk about the day's activities and ask your toddler what you need to buy at the supermarket.

Keep up the craft activities and read, read, read. When you read stories, stop before you get to the end and ask your child to guess how the story ends.

Do as much walking as possible. Your child will enjoy playing with friends at home and on the playground. On sunny days, enjoy lots of water play outdoors. Indoors, conduct "science experiments" in the bathtub by pouring and measuring water.

Start building your child's self-discipline. As parents, we need to ask: When should we turn the TV on? When does it go off? Involve your child in decision making early and you will set the foundation for personal responsibility later. Try the activities in this chapter. They are all about Learning and Loving.

1 *CONFIDENCE: Building a Little Town at Home*

• *Developmental Theme: Create and Imagine*

WHY DO IT

This activity gives young children the opportunity to stretch their imaginations, to use what they have seen outside, and to construct a little town of their own inside their home.

MATERIALS

Cardboard boxes: different sizes
Marker
Masking tape

HOW TO DO IT

With your child, gather a selection of empty, clean boxes of various sizes from your closets or get some from the store. Your child will use these boxes to construct a town.

Ask your child to line the boxes up and give them building names: "Here is the bike store. Here is the grocery store. Here is the school." You can mark the buildings and use scissors to cut windows and doors. Ask questions and play this pretend game with your child. If the boxes are big enough, your child can climb in and out of them, and talk about what's happening "in town."

ANOTHER IDEA

Encourage your child to decorate the boxes with pieces of fabric and rugs. Dolls, cars, trucks, and toys can all be brought to life in the town.

 This activity and others like it build a child's sense of independence and ownership. They are stepping stones to greater confidence.

2 CONFIDENCE: Hidden Letters
Finding letters on our foods

• *Developmental Theme: Pre-Read and Respond*

All around the kitchen there are letters: As, Bs, Fs, Ps, etc. There are letters on the soup cans, on the cat food, on the cereal box, and even on bars of soap. Bring some of these items down to your child's eye level and make a game of finding the letters. Ask your child to find two As or two Cs, or any number or combination of letters.

Start easy and build up to finding harder and harder letters. Children can point to and share the objects on which the letters have been "hidden." You're building reading observation skills as well as having fun together.

3 *CONFIDENCE: Water Magic*

• *Developmental Theme: Reach Out and Explore*

WHY DO IT

This activity teaches children about heat and cold. Experiments provide a sense of mastery.

MATERIALS

Water
Ice cube tray
Small pan

HOW TO DO IT

Make ice! With your child, fill an ice cube tray with water and place it in the freezer. Ask your child to guess when it will be frozen. Together, check to see if the water is frozen. This is an exciting moment for children.

ANOTHER IDEA

Make steam! Put a cup of water into a saucepan on the stove. Have your child stand a safe distance away, but close enough to look. Boil the water for a few minutes. The water turns into steam and goes up into the air. Your child has helped to make this happen.

 This activity can spill some water. Spread newspaper on the floor to catch the drops. Caution your child about the need for safety near the stove.

4 MOTIVATION: More and More Words

• *Developmental Theme: Pre-Read and Respond*

WHY DO IT

This activity builds vocabulary based on the everyday task of getting dressed.

MATERIALS

Everyday clothing
Large sheet of paper (as big as your child)
Marker

HOW TO DO IT

Have your child lie down on the large sheet of paper while you draw a body outline or silhouette. Write words on the silhouette for clothes and parts of the body. Tape this silhouette onto your child's bedroom wall. It's comforting for children going to bed to "see" themselves.

Say the words for clothing—shirt, pants, sock, shoe, etc. Say words for body parts—foot, arm, head, knee, etc. Then have your child say these words aloud with you.

ANOTHER IDEA

Print words for clothing and body parts on large pieces of paper. Your child, with help as needed, can attach these to the silhouette.

Play "Dress Me." This is a variation of Pin the Tail on the Donkey. While blindfolded, players pin paper cut-outs of clothes—paper shirt, shorts, socks, and shoes, etc.—onto the paper silhouette figure.

 Stop/Look/Rhyme: Sock and clock, bed and head, floor and more. Rhymes are all around us, even in the bedroom, and they're good for going to sleep and for starting on the road to reading.

5 MOTIVATION: Going Out in the World

• *Developmental Theme: Reach Out and Explore*

WHY DO IT

This activity helps children see the world around them.

HOW TO DO IT

Take a leisurely walk with your child through a shopping center. (Most of the time this is done at breakneck speed with kids being dragged along.) Show your child what goes on at the local stores. Go into the florist and watch the making of a corsage. Ask to go "backstairs" in the supermarket.

This activity is about seeing life in action outside the home. It's about exposing our children in a safe way to the larger world.

ANOTHER IDEA

To make the most of any outing, collect pictures of things your child will see along the way. You are encouraging children's curiosity to see and learn more. One idea is to match the pictures to the real things as children see them. For example, when going to the zoo, take along pictures of animals. Parents and children can make an alphabet book with these pictures.

 It doesn't need to be a fancy outing to be memorable for young children. A walk around the block or a visit to the grocery store can be as exciting as a trip to the zoo.

6 MOTIVATION: Turn the Page
Starting to read together early

• *Developmental Theme: Pre-Read and Respond*

Long before children can read, parents need to read to them and involve them with books and story telling. Reading sessions with prereaders need not be long to be significant. Ten minutes a day is fine.

Read or tell a story that poses a problem. Stop before you get to the end. Let your child put the ending to the story. Your child tells how to solve the problem.

Turn waiting time into reading time. Remember to take along story books or magazines whenever you might have to wait, such as at the doctor's office or while riding on a bus.

7 *EFFORT: Naming Toys*

• *Developmental Theme: Pre-Read and Respond*

WHY DO IT

This activity builds children's vocabulary and increases awareness of their surroundings.

HOW TO DO IT

Talk with your child about her surroundings. Try the following:

- You play with toys. Together, let's name five toys you play with: Balls? Dolls? Blocks? Action figures? Trucks? Cars? What else?
- You wear clothes. Together, let's name the clothes you wear. Shirts? Dresses? Pants? Mittens? What else?
- You eat different foods. Together, name the foods you eat. Bananas? Grapes? Milk? Pancakes? What else?

Keep these ideas going. Ask your child to test you on what you can name.

ANOTHER IDEA

Talk about and name the different things you hear and smell. Prompt your child with a few names to start, such as the aromas of flowers and noises made by clocks.

 Children need to be able to name and identify the things in the world around them. This easy activity provides both joy and mastery.

8 *EFFORT: Stepping Out with Numbers*

• *Developmental Theme: Think and Organize*

WHY DO IT

This activity helps children use numbers over an extended period of time.

MATERIALS

Paper
Marker
Ball

HOW TO DO IT

Write the numbers one through five on separate pieces of paper and review them with your child. Then place them on the floor.

Prepare a second set of numbers and ask your child to follow the directions you'll give. For example, write the number 1 on a piece of paper and hand it to your child. Ask your child to step forward one time. Then write the number 2 on a piece of paper and hand it to your child. Ask your child to step backward two times. Write the number 3 and ask your child to jump three times. Keep this activity going for as long as possible. When finished, ask your child to match the numbers with the first set of numbers on the floor.

ANOTHER IDEA

Here is an early addition problem: Bounce the ball one time. Then bounce the ball another time. Ask your child how many times the ball bounces. Trade places and let your child bounce an addition problem for you.

 So much in children's experiences today is distracting. Children need practice doing activities where they are asked to pay attention.

9 RESPONSIBILITY: Let Me, Let Me

• *Developmental Theme: Connect with Others*

WHY DO IT

Young children want to get involved and to help with chores that older children may not be eager to do. So when they say, "Let me help," let them.

MATERIALS

Stool for children to stand on
Everyday cleaning supplies
Paper/Pencil

HOW TO DO IT

With your child, think of at least one job a young child can do, with you or alone. It might be helping to set the table, feeding the pet, or picking up newspapers. Make a list of the jobs your child suggests.

Write the jobs on a piece of paper and post it where you and your child can see it. Pick a time of day when a job can be done. Change jobs every few days so that your child gets a variety of experiences.

ANOTHER IDEA

Let your child help with some safe mealtime chores, such as mixing items in a bowl, placing cold foods on plates, and wiping the table. If they stand safely on a stool, children can reach and help from an early age.

 When it's time for the task to be completed, ask "How is the job coming? When will you be finished?" Expect an adequate job, not a perfect one. Show children how to do a good job, yet resist redoing it yourself.

10 *RESPONSIBILITY: Early Years Safety First*
Helping children learn to be healthy and safe

• *Developmental Theme: Promote Good Daily Habits*

Young children who have learned how to dial 911 can save lives—their own and those of their family. Children who learn the habit of washing their hands well can often keep illness at bay. Children who learn with you the way to cross a street safely will tend to follow those rules when they are on their own later.

Show your child how to dial 911 and then practice it (hold down on the phone's hang up button so the call does not actually go out). Some children may want to do more with the phone such as place a call to grandma.

Practice washing hands with soap, rinsing, and wiping dry. This combines children's love of water with an important health routine.

Cross a nearby street showing how to follow the color-coded street light: Go, Caution, Stop. Then, you may want to try crossing at the corner without a light. Check to see how your child has understood the caution that needs to be taken for crossing alone later on.

11 INITIATIVE: We Lead Each Other

• *Developmental Theme: Pre-Read and Respond*

WHY DO IT

Here's an active game that combines listening to and giving directions, using lots of words.

HOW TO DO IT

Your and your child take turns being the leader. For the first round, the parent is the leader. As the leader, give your child (the follower) a direction, such as "Take three big steps." The leader can also ask the follower to pretend to be a car or a train or a teacher, or to be noisy or quiet, for example.

Then the leader and follower change places. The new leader (your child) gives you directions. It might be to talk very loud or to whisper. It might be to lie down or to stand tall. The follower does it, and the game continues.

ANOTHER IDEA

Add dance to the directions. Put on the radio and the fun goes on. The sounds of music complement the sounds of words.

 Youngsters who do a lot of talking at home tend to achieve more in school. Connecting words to real experiences are great ways to remember words and concepts.

12 INITIATIVE: Hot, Cold, Light, Shadow
Learning science basics easily

• Developmental Theme: Reach Out and Explore

Water and light are great natural wonders and teachers of science. Try these easy and delightful experiments:

Evaporation—Put some water in an open dish and put it in a sunny place. Let your child put a mark where the water level was at first. Use another dish with an equal amount of water, but put it in a shady place. Watch what happens to the water levels each day.

Hot and cold—On a warm, sunny day, lay some wet clothes outside. Put some in the sun, some in the shade. Talk about which ones dry first and why.

Light and shadow—When are shadows longer and shorter during the day? Try making different shadows using your hands, sticks, pots, and pans. Let your child match the movements and shadows of others when they jump, skip, wave hands, and wiggle feet.

13 INITIATIVE: From Different Angles

• *Developmental Theme: Reach Out and Explore*

WHY DO IT
This activity helps us look and find what we otherwise might not see.

MATERIALS
Old blanket

HOW TO DO IT
During the day and especially at dusk, lie on your back with your child and look up at clouds, trees, branches, and stars. Spread out a blanket for your comfort.

Lie on your stomach and look down at things from an animal's point of view. Look at plants and stones for colors, patterns, curves, lines. Look for shapes—squares, circles, triangles. Look for the same thing in different sizes—twigs, clouds, and leaves.

ANOTHER IDEA
Check different places in the mud or snow for animal tracks. Make tracks in the mud and snow to see what your shoeprints look like.

 Talk with your child about what you have both observed. There are many ways of experiencing our environment. This helps us understand and remember more.

14 PERSEVERANCE: Labeling Home Objects
Helping children recognize words

• *Developmental Theme: Pre-Read and Respond*

Just as in the schoolroom where teachers label doors and desks, a great game for parents and youngsters at home is to label the bed, sofa, rugs, etc. Use big, bold print lettering and masking tape to hang your labels on the walls and furniture (masking tape won't leave marks).

Say the words aloud together. Enjoy these games and others you make up with your child. Learning to read is a great adventure.

15 PERSEVERANCE: Can and Carton Numbers
Getting acquainted with numbers

• *Developmental Theme: Think and Organize*

Numbers, Numbers Everywhere—Just as with letters, numbers are all around your home, especially in the kitchen. Look for numbers and talk about them with your child. Once you start looking, you will find them everywhere.

Can Numbers—Save those empty, clean soup cans. Strip off the wrappers and paste number labels on different cans. You might have a row of one to ten. Now you're ready for anything from just identifying the number itself to more complicated adding and subtracting. Pick two cans. Add the numbers together to get a total. Pick another two cans, and subtract the smaller number from the larger number. You can also paste macaroni on each can in the shape of the number to make the game more "tactile" for young children.

Egg Carton Counter—Find an old egg carton and write a number in the bottom of each section. Then use little pieces of paper or pennies (anything small) to match the number in the section with the right number of items.

16 CARING: New and Old Toys
Finding new uses for objects

• *Developmental Theme: Create and Imagine*

The best toys are those that can be used in multiple ways. That's why blocks and building toys are often preferable to cars and trucks, which can usually do only one thing. Help your child realize that some of the best and most versatile toys are those he already has right at home.

For example, consider a paper plate and a rubber band.

Ask, how many different ways can we use a paper plate? Start the conversation going. As a dish, but what else? Soon the plate, thanks to your child's imagination, will be a hat, a Frisbee, and much more—ideas well beyond what you yourself might imagine.

And think of that lowly rubber band. What can it do and how does it work with the paper plate to make lots of new things?

Keep going. You already have many items at home that are really great toys.

17 CARING: Letter to My Child
Showing children how much they are loved

• *Developmental Theme: Think and Organize*

Parents, gather your thoughts for an activity called Letter to My Child.

Think about what you would like to tell your child about yourself, what you care about (your values), and how much you care about your child (your love, concern, affection).

Make this letter easy to write. Jot down the phrases as you think of them, and gather as many of your ideas as possible in advance. Then write the letter. Read it aloud to your child. Save it in a scrapbook to be looked at years later.

18 CARING: Pictures Tell The Story

• Developmental Theme: Create and Imagine

WHY DO IT
This activity uses pictures to help children learn more about their families.

MATERIALS
Photographs of your child and other family members
Magazines with pictures of people

HOW TO DO IT
Give your child several family photographs to look at. Ask your child to choose a photo of a family activity, look at it carefully, and then turn it over.

Then ask your child questions about the picture. For example:
- Who is in the picture?
- What is the person wearing?
- Is the person outdoors or indoors?
- What else do you see?

Then tell your child three activities that you enjoy. For example, biking, swimming, and reading. Ask your child to repeat the names of these three activities.

Finally, ask your child to name two activities she likes. Talk about these.

ANOTHER IDEA
Find and cut out three pictures from magazines or newspapers of families doing activities together. With your child, arrange and paste them on a large sheet of paper. This is a family poster. Use words to describe the pictures.

 We hope that our children recognize the caring of their families. Just in case, take a moment to tell your child how members of your family care for each other.

19 *TEAMWORK: Doing Chores Together*
Helping children work with you

• *Developmental Theme: Connect with Others*

Most children actually enjoy house and outdoor chores when they do them with their parents. Make doing chores fun by working as a team. One person can sweep or vacuum while the other person dusts.

Baking is another task that is more fun to do as a team. When two or more people bake together, the result can be a more creative and tasty batch of cookies.

There is something special about being in the same place, doing a job together. This isn't just to keep an eye on children; it's to build the spirit of accomplishing a task together.

20 TEAMWORK: Helping Plants Grow

• *Developmental Theme: Think and Organize*

WHY DO IT

This activity helps children begin, continue, and complete a project. In this activity, a plant grows from seed to flower.

MATERIALS

Two packages of seeds
Dirt
Water and a big spoon
Plastic cups with holes in the bottom

HOW TO DO IT

For a garden indoors or out, obtain seeds with pictures on the packets. Consider carrot or radish seeds because they sprout quickly. Use your spoon to fill the cups with dirt and plant the seeds. As the plants grow, let your child do lots of the work, weeding and watering.

   Look at the plants together every day to check their progress.

ANOTHER IDEA

Your child can share one or more of these plants with a friend or relative. Plants have a way of showing "We love you, and we care."

 Children need to be part of the family team. Think of projects to do together, such as baking a cake or raking the yard.

21 COMMON SENSE: I Remember

• *Developmental Theme: Create and Imagine*

WHY DO IT

Knowing how to recall and use information from past events, even from yesterday or this morning, is an important building block for common sense. This activity provides that practice.

HOW TO DO IT

Ask your child questions such as:

- What did you eat for breakfast this morning? What did you eat for supper last night? What do you wish that you had eaten? or …What would you like to eat?
- What sock do you put on first? Ask your child to point to the foot.
- What shirt did you wear yesterday? Ask your child to find it (it might be in the laundry). What color shirt do you like best?

Trade places. Let your child tell you what he wants you to remember. Make a mistake now and then so he can catch you.

ANOTHER IDEA

After you have read the first few pages of a book to your child, stop and ask questions. Ask easier ones such as, "What color shirt was the boy wearing?" as well as harder ones, such as "What do you think is going to happen next?"

Encourage and expand on your child's memories, even fantasies. Children may say they traveled to the sun yesterday. Fine, you can say, "Yes, I went with you and this is what I saw…What did you see?"

22 COMMON SENSE: Sit, Sit
Helping children practice self-discipline

• *Developmental Theme: Promote Good Daily Habits*

While today's classrooms don't require children to sit at their desks all day, much of the work is done sitting down. Young children, unaccustomed to having their bottoms on chairs, have to get used to it when they begin school. You can give them some early practice by playing this game.

Gather some chairs and a watch or clock with a second hand, if possible.

Play a version of musical chairs in which once you sit down, you have to stay seated for a certain period of time. Start with a fifteen-second sit-down. Then move toward thirty seconds, then one minute. Have a goal of at least a three-minute sit-down. During this time you can talk or read or just sit quietly together.

23 PROBLEM SOLVING: Bye, Bye Fear
Talking together about fear

• *Developmental Theme: Connect with Others*

Everybody has fears. As we grow older, we learn ways to cope with them. Children need to talk about fears without becoming more fearful.

First, let your child tell you what scares her. Try not to say "That's so silly." Tell your child about fears you had as a child, about the monster under the bed who turned out not to be a monster after all. Talk about situations that made you fearful. Maybe you were scared of big dogs.

When children are scared of dogs, it's helpful to have a friendly dog nearby for your child to pet. Even without that, books and stories about dogs will help too.

24 PROBLEM SOLVING: I'm Thinking!

• *Developmental Theme: Think and Organize*

WHY DO IT

This activity enables your young child to listen for and use clues found around the house. Using clues is an important observation and problem solving skill.

HOW TO DO IT

Begin by saying, "I'm thinking of something in this room. Can you guess what it is?" Then give hints one at a time that describe your surprise object—color, size, or use. For example, if you're thinking about a saucer, you could use hints like these: "It's the size of a pancake, it's blue and white, and it's often used under a cup."

After each clue ask your child to guess the object.

Then switch places with your child. Let him give you clues for you to guess.

ANOTHER IDEA

Use a blindfold to add excitement and build your child's and your memory about what's in the room. Move throughout the house and describe objects in other rooms.

 This is a particularly good activity to play while waiting in a doctor's office or in line at a supermarket. It also works well during a long automobile trip: "Let's look out the window and see what we can see."

25　PROBLEM SOLVING: "Time-Out" for Toys
Helping children talk it over

• *Developmental Theme: Listen, Speak, and Do*

Children sometimes disagree about who is going to play with what toy. If this happens, give the toy a "time-out" for five minutes.

Ask your children to try to solve a problem by identifying possible solutions. After five minutes, if the dispute is not settled, retire the toy for the rest of the day. Bring the toy back out the next day. Chances are, the problem will have evaporated.

26 PROBLEM SOLVING: TV Time—Yes or No?

• *Developmental Theme: Promote Good Daily Habits*

WHY DO IT

Decisions need to be made about what times and for how long children can watch TV, even at the youngest of ages. Similar rules may be needed for the computer.

MATERIALS

TV Guide
Pencil/Marker

HOW TO DO IT

Decide together how much TV your family will watch. Read the TV schedule. Have each family member decide what he or she would like to watch. Put initials next to everyone's choices. Do this for the youngest child also.

Decide what you will watch each day or week. Circle your choices. If two people want to watch different programs at the same time, try to compromise. Take turns.

Try to find time to watch TV with your child. Be sure she understands what's real and what isn't.

ANOTHER IDEA

Have board games, books, or projects handy so children can do other things when TV time is used up.

Most children watch too much TV. If your child watches too much, try cutting down a little at a time. Avoid leaving a TV set on all day.

See Our TV Plan in Chapter Nine: Opening School Doors for another version of this activity.

27 FOCUS: Walk the Line

• *Developmental Theme: Reach Out and Explore*

WHY DO IT

This activity builds physical coordination through easy-to-do practice.

HOW TO DO IT

Hands and Feet: Practice standing on one foot at a time. This isn't easy. Place your chin on your chest and close your eyes. Next, balance on tiptoes. Have your child put both hands and feet on the floor. Then, tell him to lift his left hand, left foot, and right foot, one at a time. Try this yourself.

Your Body: Talk with your child about motions that can be made with different parts of the body. Then try them. For example, blink, wiggle, nod, tap, clap, shake, walk, run, jump, hop, climb, etc.

ANOTHER IDEA

Eyes and Hands: Drop clothespins into a bottle or throw beanbags into a pail or wastebasket. For young children, put the basket or pail in back of the sofa. In this way, children can lean comfortably over the sofa and aim from above.

 Draw a chalk line on the sidewalk. Ask your child to walk the line without stepping off. Make other lines—a crooked line, a square, a circle, a triangle, a rectangle. Let your child draw his own lines also.

28 FOCUS: In the Bag

• *Developmental Theme: Listen, Speak, and Do*

WHY DO IT

This activity helps children learn new words and practice following and giving directions.

MATERIALS

Large paper grocery bag

HOW TO DO IT

Open the grocery bag and place it on the floor. Ask your child to listen to you and follow these directions, one at a time:

- Stand beside the bag.
- Step over the bag.
- Put one foot inside the bag.
- Take one foot out of the bag.
- Walk around the bag.
- Put the bag under a chair.

ANOTHER IDEA

Trade places. Let your child give you directions about how to use the bag. Children love giving parents instructions to follow.

 This is an ideal activity for giving parents needed time to unwind after a long day at work. Parents can relax on the sofa while children listen and follow this direction game.

29 *FOCUS: Watch Carefully*

• *Developmental Theme: Reach Out and Explore*

WHY DO IT

Learning to watch and observe are key ingredients in a child's later academic success, especially in science.

HOW TO DO IT

Look for machines around the house. Take a look at the furnace, if you can. Talk about how it works. What are all those connections and pipes for?

This needn't turn into a complicated explanation, unless parents and children are really interested. What it offers on a less scholarly level is an exercise in observation and a feel for how things work.

ANOTHER IDEA

Don't forget to talk about those plumbing pipes. It really is a shame that some are not exposed so that children can see the activity beneath the walls.

Science can be found outside the house as well as inside. Catching salamanders and putting insects in bottles are scientific doings, people exploring their environment. Sitting on the front porch watching the clouds move is also part of science and a necessary first step toward future interests of both boys and girls.

30 *RESPECT: Happy and Sad*
Learning about feelings

• *Developmental Theme: Personal Competency*

Even young children have a sense of what makes them happy and what makes them sad. With your child, talk first about what makes people happy. Is it being with a child? A sunny day? A call from a friend?

Then ask about what makes people sad. Is it a rainy day? Is it a baby who is crying? Is the baby feeling sick?

Tell your child what makes you happy. Tell your child what makes you feel sad. Ask your child to name one thing that makes her feel happy. What makes her feel sad? It might be exactly what you just said, and that's fine.

The goal is to get feelings expressed and out in the open. When children get a sense of what they feel, they can gain a better sense of what others feel.

31 *RESPECT: Wait, Wait*
Helping children develop patience

• *Developmental Theme: Personal Competency*

In a small household, it's easy for children to get the idea that whenever they want to talk, they talk. Whenever they want something, they ask for it and get it. You want your child to speak up, but you also need to provide practice in waiting to speak and waiting to get needs met.

Here is a fun and useful mealtime exercise. Everyone gets a chance to talk about a subject of mutual interest, such as food, television, friends, and so on. The point is to get young children (and older ones, too) in the habit of listening to others and of taking turns. Start with thirty seconds of talking followed by thirty seconds of listening time, and move up to one minute, two at most.

32 RESPECT: Saying It So It Works
Building good behavior

• Developmental Theme: Promote Good Daily Habits

Young children know when parents mean it. Before we tell children what will happen if they misbehave, we have to be prepared to follow through. When we say, "No TV for a week," we had better mean it, or not say it.

As with everyone else, children behave better when they feel special and needed. When we ask even young children to pick up toys, nagging does not work nearly as well as saying "You know how to make things tidy. Let's straighten up the room together."

39 Activities

7

Moving Forward: Ages 3–4 Years

"Children nowadays are tyrants. They contradict their parents, gobble their food and tyrannize their teachers."
— Socrates

ACTIVITY	DEVELOPMENTAL THEME
Getting It Together	Listen, Speak, and Do
Word Train	Pre-Read and Respond
Make Beautiful Music	Create and Imagine
More Than One	Reach Out and Explore
Collecting Clouds	Think and Organize
Few Good Words	Promote Good Daily Habits
Sign Signals	Pre-Read and Respond
Number Stitching	Personal Competency
Letters in My Name	Pre-Read and Respond
It Reminds Me Of	Pre-Read and Respond
Word "Fish"	Create and Imagine
Coin Counting	Listen, Speak, and Do
Keeping Healthy	Promote Good Daily Habits
Fill the Button Hole	Promote Good Daily Habits
Pennies Add Up	Reach Out and Explore
Math on the Move	Listen, Speak, and Do
Puzzle Pleasure	Personal Competency
Roomfuls of Words	Think and Organize
Shaping Up	Create and Imagine
Spaghetti Letters	Create and Imagine
You Be Me	Connect with Others
Talk Through	Listen, Speak, and Do
Telephone Charm	Listen, Speak, and Do
Crew Duties	Think and Organize
Finding Treasures Together	Reach Out and Explore
What Happens Next?	Pre-Read and Respond

• Welcome to Moving Forward

Children are taking big steps at this age. They are having conversations with you and becoming more interesting and enterprising every day. Share your own childhood experiences and tell your child about what it was like when he was a baby.

Your child is now playing with friends and with you in a more grown up way. You are sharing the pleasures of reading, telling your children about what you read and why you liked it. You talk about your favorite TV shows and ask about theirs.

Check out your local community resources. Take your child to library story hours and to pick out books. Take long walks and talk about everything you see. Ask for your child's opinions.

Your child is beginning to understand why sometimes you have to say no and is becoming a little more grown-up everyday.

Try the activities in this chapter. They are all about Learning and Loving.

1 *CONFIDENCE: Getting It Together*

• *Developmental Theme: Listen, Speak, and Do*

WHY DO IT
This activity teaches colors, sensory skills (touch), shapes, and sizes.

MATERIALS
Cloth scraps
Yarn
Buttons
Paper plates
Macaroni
Glue or paste
Lace
Beans

HOW TO DO IT
Have your child arrange pieces of material on a paper plate. She can glue the pieces on the paper plate and add other materials such as macaroni and lace until she feels it's finished.

Talk with your child about the materials used for the collage. Ask your child to name the materials used.

Punch a hole through the edge of the plate and use yarn or string to hang the collage as you would hang a picture.

ANOTHER IDEA
Make several collages, each with a different theme. Hang these collages on long strings from the ceiling of your child's room. These decorations will move and delight.

 To make lots of artwork at home, keep a general junk box of materials on hand, such as cardboard rolls, old sewing spools, bottle caps, etc., to spark your child's imagination. For older children, keep magazines, books, games, or cards on hand. Children are creative. Parents are too!

2 *CONFIDENCE: Word Train*
Helping children build vocabulary

• *Developmental Theme: Pre-Read and Respond*

As you child learns new words, make a "train" of these words across the wall of your child's room. Write each word on a piece of paper, and add a new "car" each time a new word is learned.

As your child falls asleep, he can play a game with all the words he knows. He can look at and recall all the words each day. Try to add a new word daily.

Ask your child to join with you and repeat the words he knows quietly and gently. Repeating the words helps children relax as they go to sleep.

3 *CONFIDENCE: Make Beautiful Music*
Helping children create and share

• *Developmental Theme: Create and Imagine*

All the world is a stage. Use pots, wooden spoons, shakers, and small kitchen utensils to have a musical performance. Ask children to tell stories, sing, do tricks, and parade while playing instruments. Spread out a sheet or blanket for guests to use as "seats" in the backyard or at the park. Ask your child to create "tickets" for those who will attend the big event. Invite other children to come, bring their instruments, and perform.

4 *CONFIDENCE: More Than One*

Helping children recognize words that mean "more than one"

• *Developmental Theme: Reach Out and Explore*

Gather pairs of things from around the house: shoes, mittens, socks, earrings, etc. Ask your child to find other things that come in pairs and bring them to you.

Print the word for one object in the pair on a piece of paper (for example, "shoe"). Then print the word for the name of the pair on another piece of paper ("shoes"). Mix the papers together. Have your child choose one and bring you the object that corresponds to the paper. When the paper says "shoe" your child will bring one shoe. When the paper says "shoes," the child will get two shoes.

5 MOTIVATION: Collecting Clouds

• Developmental Theme: Think and Organize

WHY DO IT
This activity uses creativity and expands thinking skills.

MATERIALS
White paper
Colored paper
Glue
Marker or pencil

HOW TO DO IT
Lie down outdoors with your child. Look at the clouds that pass overhead and take turns imagining what the shapes look like: animals, buildings, trees, etc. Take turns making up stories about the cloud shapes as well.

Ask your child to tear some sheets of white paper into the shapes of clouds. Then ask her to tell you what she sees. Glue the cloud shapes onto colored paper. Under the clouds help your child write, "My cloud looks like…" Post these pictures for family members to enjoy.

ANOTHER IDEA
On the back of the page, help your child write a sentence or two about the clouds. Have family members guess what your child thinks the cloud shapes look like.

 Resolve to try to spend some uninterrupted time with your child. Five minutes a day is a good start.

6 *MOTIVATION: A Few Good Words*
Helping children stay healthy

• *Developmental Theme: Promote Good Daily Habits*

Post messages for your child at home, near places where good health habits need to be practiced. Family members can write and post messages for each other to follow.

Next to the sink, post the message "Please wash your hands before eating." A picture message for hand washing can show hands, soap, and a sink.

Designate a personal shelf or shoebox in the bathroom or bedroom to hold your child's health care items. These can include soap, comb, brush, toothbrush, and toothpaste.

7 *MOTIVATION: Sign Signals*
Helping children "read" the world outside

• *Developmental Theme: Pre-read and Respond*

Identifying and reading signs helps children to know their neighborhood and be aware of symbols that keep them safe.

Go for a walk with your child to try to find as many street signs as you can: signs that say Stop, Walk, and Bus Stop. When you return home, together use paper and marker to draw and label the signs you saw. Point to each sign and have your child identify it.

8 EFFORT: Number Stitching

• *Developmental Theme: Personal Competency*

WHY DO IT
This activity teaches children to form numbers and build physical coordination through stitching to make a lovely design.

MATERIALS
Heavy paper such as cardboard
Colored yarn
Tape
Scissors
Pencil

HOW TO DO IT
Write a large number on a piece of cardboard. Punch holes through the number at different places. Take a piece of colored yarn and attach a small piece of tape around both ends. Help your child pull the yarn through the holes in the cardboard and "stitch" the design.

   This takes effort and results in a product that both children and parents can be proud of.

ANOTHER IDEA
Write letters instead of numbers on the cardboard. Children enjoy stitching their names. You do some too. These make attractive wall decorations.

 Give sewing work as gifts. For example, hand-sewn bookmarks, toy animals, felt banners, potholders, and placemats make excellent gifts. (Note: If you use a needle for this activity, show your child how to use it safely.)

9 *EFFORT: Letters in My Name*

• *Developmental Theme: Pre-Read and Respond*

WHY DO IT

This activity develops letter recognition, small muscle development, and eye-hand coordination.

MATERIALS

Old magazines (large ones)
Paper
Scissors
Paste
Crayons

HOW TO DO IT

Print your child's first name on a piece of paper. Then have your child search the magazines for large letters that match his name and cut them out. Paste one letter on each page. Talk about each letter and help your child think about and say words that begin with that letter. Incorporate the letter you have discussed into a crayon drawing.

ANOTHER IDEA

Pick another member of the family and have your child search in magazines for print letters to spell that person's name. Find examples of those special letters. Have your child cut the letters out and paste the letters onto a page.

 Learning how to spell one's name is an important personal step and a school success skill.

10 EFFORT: It Reminds Me Of…
Helping children make connections

• *Developmental Theme: Pre-Read and Respond*

Word association is a beginning reading skill. Word pairs help your child to identify things that go together. Make a game of asking your child to tell you what word goes with each of the following:

sock	(shoe)
hat	(glove)
fire	(smoke)
hand	(foot)

Each word also has a number of other words that can go with it. Ask your child to add to the list. Accept your child's answers when they are workable. Let your child have a turn naming words for you to match.

11 EFFORT: Word "Fish"
Building recognition of words

• *Developmental Theme: Create and Imagine*

Tell your child, "We are going fishing. Before we can fish, we must have bait, so we are going to dig for our worms."

The "worms" are pictures with words found in magazines and newspapers. Continue finding pictures until you have at least five "worms" in the can.

When all the worms are in the can, say to your child, "Now we are ready to go fishing." Say the name of the picture and ask your child to find the word. When all the "fish" are caught, you can start again, finding pictures to add to the worm can.

To add complexity, you can play the same game with beginning and ending sounds of words.

12 RESPONSIBILITY: Coin Counting
Helping children build saving habits

• *Developmental Theme: Listen, Speak, and Do*

Empty leftover change into a small dish. Point out each coin to your child and say how much it is worth. Ask your child to identify the coins. When your child guesses the right coin, it can go into a piggy bank.

After a while (pick your time frame), help your child empty the bank and count the money. Make a list of the coins withdrawn from the bank. Your child can choose what the money will be used for.

This teaches your child the differences between coins, and it starts good saving habits.

13 RESPONSIBILITY: Keeping Healthy

• *Developmental Theme: Promote Good Habits*

WHY DO IT
Parents and children need to discuss basic health habits.

MATERIALS
Paper
Marker
Magazines with pictures of people doing activities

HOW TO DO IT
Look with your child through magazines to find pictures of people using good health habits. Examples include brushing teeth, washing and eating vegetables, cleaning fingernails, and wearing boots on a wet day.

Talk about, cut out, and post these pictures in different rooms of the house, such as the bathroom and kitchen.

ANOTHER IDEA
List three health reminders in big letters. For example, "Wear your sweater. It's chilly today. I love you."

 Even before children can read, they like to receive messages. Post messages to your child for all to see. Your child can practice saying the words aloud.

14 RESPONSIBILITY: Fill the Button Hole

• *Developmental Theme: Promote Good Daily Habits*

WHY DO IT

This activity teaches your child to button and unbutton clothes correctly and without help.

MATERIALS

A piece of material or sleeve that has buttonholes and buttons in it.

HOW TO DO IT

With your child watching, demonstrate how to match a button with a buttonhole. Guide your child's hand to pull the buttons through the holes. Repeat these actions several times.

Let your child show off by practicing with your buttons.

ANOTHER IDEA

Count the number of buttons. Then cover up two buttons. How many are left? What color are the buttons? Do some adding or subtracting with the different buttons.

 Put together a child's sewing box. Include different colors of thread, a few buttons, tape measure, a needle, and a few pins. Show your child how to use sharp objects safely.

See page 154 for a related activity, "Scratch and Fix."

15 *RESPONSIBILITY: Pennies Add Up*
Helping children build interest in math and ability to use coins

• *Developmental Theme: Reach Out and Explore*

Show your child a penny. Ask how many cents a penny is worth. Show a nickel. Place five pennies next to the nickel. Tell your child that five pennies are the same as a nickel. Show your child two nickels and a dime. Talk about how these are equal. Now add the number of pennies needed to equal two nickels or one dime.

Play "store" with your child. Pull out three grocery items from the cupboard and make up low-cost prices of each, something like five cents, eight cents, and eleven cents. Put the prices on pieces of paper next to the items. Now your child can go "shopping" by counting the coins needed to buy the items.

ANOTHER IDEA

On another day, move to "big money." Show your child a quarter. Using pennies, nickels, and dimes, ask your child to count out a quarter in different ways.

16 INITIATIVE: Math on the Move

• *Developmental Theme: Listen, Speak, and Do*

WHY DO IT

This activity helps children get more comfortable with numbers. Children and parents exercise at the same time.

MATERIALS

A ball that bounces
Pencil
Paper
Wristwatch
Radio or CD player

HOW TO DO IT

This is an exercise plan you do with your child

Day One: Bounce the ball five times. Jump in place five times. Jog for one minute.

Day Two: Bounce the ball ten times. Jump in place ten times. Jog for two minutes.

Day Three: Bounce the ball fifteen times. Jump in place fifteen times. Jog for three minutes.

Time each other. Count to be sure that each of you does your part. You can choose to add music while you are exercising.

ANOTHER IDEA

Get other members of the family to participate in these exercises. Have a contest. Give your child a watch or clock. Soon she will be timing everything, including the time needed for the daily exercise.

Games at home are a good way to help children get used to routines and learn to follow rules. Set regular times for games. These might be a half hour after lunch or dinner. This puts scheduling into children's days and teaches get-ready-for-school skills.

17 INITIATIVE: Puzzle Pleasure

• *Developmental Theme: Personal Competency*

WHY DO IT
This activity teaches organizing with wholes and parts.

MATERIALS
Magazine picture or child's drawing
Paste or glue
Cardboard or heavy paper
Pencil or crayon
Scissors

HOW TO DO IT
Find a magazine picture or one of your child's drawings. With your child, paste it onto cardboard and trim the excess. Turn the cardboard over and with your child draw five to eight large pieces. Cut the pattern into sections. Then scramble the parts. Have your child put the pieces together to make the whole picture.

ANOTHER IDEA
Make several puzzles. Mix the pieces together and ask your child to assemble each puzzle. Decrease the size and increase the number of puzzle pieces as your child gains skill in assembling parts into the whole.

 Help your child learn to make do with what you can afford. You may not be able to afford elaborate toys, but you can buy a pack of cards that your child can use to play hundreds of games. Instead of a fancy toy, substitute something far more enduring for your child—your imagination and your time!

18 *INITIATIVE: Roomfuls of Words*

Helping children build observation skills

• *Developmental Theme: Think and Organize*

Divide large sheets of paper into sections labeled "living room," "bedroom," "kitchen," etc. Look in newspapers and magazines for pictures of furniture and other objects that belong in different rooms of the house. Ask your child to cut out and paste the pictures of the furniture that fit into the different rooms. Help your child label each piece of furniture in the room. Put these words on cards and review them often.

See page 133 for an extended version of this activity.

19 PERSEVERANCE: *Shaping Up*

• *Developmental Theme: Create and Imagine*

WHY DO IT

This activity helps children recognize shapes in everyday objects and builds observation skills important to school success.

MATERIALS

Paper
Pencil

HOW TO DO IT

Explain to your child that shapes can be recognized in everyday objects. Together pick out these shapes: circles in traffic lights, a triangle in a "yield" sign, squares in tile floors, and rectangles in windows. Ask your child to find two other examples of each shape.

Draw and talk about each of these shapes: circle, square, rectangle, and triangle. Be sure to explain how they differ. Ask your child to draw each of the shapes.

ANOTHER IDEA

Encourage your child to design pictures by combining shapes to make objects such as a house (triangle, square) or wagon (rectangles, four circles).

Help your child draw and cut out shapes from paper. Label each shape.

 Children like to see their work displayed. Using yarn or string, hang the shapes as a mobile. Use you child's artwork as decorations for a party, or make placemats using shapes. You and your child can write guests' names and draw pictures on the mats.

20 PERSEVERANCE: Spaghetti Letters
Helping your child name and create the letters of the alphabet

• *Developmental Theme: Create and Imagine*

Cook and drain one cup of spaghetti that has been broken into two to three inch pieces. Place spaghetti in a bowl with cool water to keep it from sticking together. Have a cookie sheet or other flat surface ready.

Make a list of alphabet letters on a piece of paper: Aa, Bb, Cc, etc. Name an alphabet letter and have your child point to the letter that you name. Using a piece of spaghetti, ask your child to form the letter you named.

Give help if needed. The spaghetti is wiggly so letters will not be perfect. See how many letters you can each make in ten minutes.

21 CARING: You Be Me
Helping children "see" themselves

• *Developmental Theme: Connect with Others*

Trading places (which we do often in MegaSkills activities) is one way to help young children start to see themselves from another person's point of view.

In this activity, parents take the lead. Say, "Now I am going to act like my little child. I am going to eat like my child and walk like my child and talk like my child." Your child will watch and howl with delight.

The idea is not to make fun of your child, but to show him with lots of love what he looks like in his parent's eyes. He may even get the idea of saying: "Now, I am going to act like my mom."

22 CARING: Talk Through

Helping children use words, not fists

• *Developmental Theme: Listen, Speak, and Do*

Sometimes it is hard for children to control their emotions. They may lash out at another child even as they're playing. When you're nearby, use red light, yellow light, and green light signals with your child. These can be circles cut from paper or words displayed where children play.

A green light signal indicates things are okay. A yellow light signal means you are giving a warning that something is not going well. A red light signal means stop; we are going to talk about the problem.

23 CARING: Telephone Charm

Communicating information to others

• *Developmental Theme: Listen, Speak, and Do*

When you need to call a relative or friend, ask your child to dial the number. You can prearrange a good time with friends and give them a few questions they can ask your child.

Write down the telephone number on a piece of paper. Explain to your child that you should dial the first number starting on the left, then the next one, until you reach the last number. Ask your child to wait until someone answers, and then say, "Hello, this is _____ calling. May I please speak to _____?"

The adult on the phone can ask questions of your child such as, "How are you today? What are you planning to do? Are you looking forward to something that will happen soon?" Suggest that the adult ask questions that can't be answered with a simple yes or no, so your child can practice communication skills.

Prepare your child in advance by practicing asking and answering questions. Practice saying, "Thank you for calling," at the end of the conversation.

24 *TEAMWORK: Crew Duties*

Making chores fun

• *Developmental Theme: Think and Organize*

Cleaning Closets: Make a game out of cleaning a closet. Divide the job into parts. Explain that you will clean the closet floor first and do the rest of the closet another day.

Make a game of getting everything off the closet floor. For example, race each other to see who gets the shoes out faster. Dust the floor. Then take turns to see who gets the shoes into the closet faster. Remember to count and pair the shoes.

Folding Towels: Fold and store towels together on laundry day. Show your child how to fold. Try not to redo your child's work. Even the youngest pre-schooler can fold smaller towels. When the job is finished, ask your child what was accomplished. Ask what other household job your child would like to try, and give her a chance to be successful with a new chore.

Helping with jobs around the house builds a child's can-do skills.

25 TEAMWORK: Finding Treasures Together

• *Developmental Theme: Reach Out and Explore*

WHY DO IT

Schools require children to work together and cooperate. Yet perseverance is often first learned and practiced at home.

MATERIALS

Paper bag

HOW TO DO IT

Have an outdoor treasure hunt. Think of a short list of items to find such as a small stone, branch, or a green or red leaf. Give your child a paper bag for the collection. Add excitement by timing the minutes it takes to find the objects.

ANOTHER IDEA

Use the treasure hunt idea when you go grocery shopping. Your child may be able to help you point to needed items on the lower shelves at the supermarket.

 Turn chores into games of perseverance. For example, when picking up toys, see how many toys both of you can pick up and put away in two minutes. Keep track of the time. How well did you do? What else needs to be picked up?

26 TEAMWORK: What Happens Next?

• *Developmental Theme: Pre-Read and Respond*

WHY DO IT

This activity teaches new vocabulary and enriches your child's awareness.

MATERIALS

A storybook that has many repetitions, such as "The Old Woman and Her Pig," "The Three Billy Goats Gruff," "The Three Pigs," or "The Three Bears."

HOW TO DO IT

Read a story to your child. Read the story again. Give your child an opportunity to participate by stopping before the most-repeated lines. Ask your child to supply the next line of the story. When he is very familiar with the story, stop more and more frequently.

ANOTHER IDEA

After the story has been read over many times, ask your child to tell you the story. Read the story again and ask him to tell you another way the story might develop and add a new ending.

 Encourage your child to listen for story repetitions and think about alternative endings. This helps to develop reading, speaking, and thinking skills that are vital for language development.

27 COMMON SENSE: Which One Is It?

• *Developmental Theme: Think and Organize*

WHY DO IT

This activity develops practical knowledge for everyday living and helps your child think before making judgments.

MATERIALS

Containers of various sizes
Water
Measuring cup

HOW TO DO IT

Ask your child to fill containers of various sizes with water poured from a measuring cup. Place the containers into three groups: those that hold more water than one measuring cup, those that hold less, and those that hold the same.

Look at the shapes of the containers. Ask your child, "Do the tall containers always hold the most water? Do the short containers always hold less water?"

Put two containers next to each other. Ask your child to guess which one will hold the most water. Have your child pour water into both containers and check her guess.

ANOTHER IDEA

Use the measuring cup to practice finding how many quarter cups or half cups it takes to make one cup. How many quarter or half cups does it take to make two cups?

 Children like to make choices between alternatives and test to see if their guesses are correct. When children practice weighing possible solutions, they strengthen their ability to use their common sense.

28 COMMON SENSE: Checking First
Helping children prevent problems

• Developmental Theme: Personal Competency

Show your child how you check first before doing certain activities. For example, "I check to make sure there is a saucer under the plant before I water it." Or, "Before I climb this ladder, I check to see that it is in good condition."

Ask your child to think of what to check on before doing an activity. Examples: Check the temperature of the shower or bath water before getting into the tub. Check to see if clothes for the next day are clean.

Checking first before doing something is common sense practice.

29 COMMON SENSE: Where Does It Belong?

• *Developmental Theme: Think and Organize*

WHY DO IT
This activity gives your child practice sorting and classifying.

MATERIALS
Magazine pictures of furniture items
Paper
Glue or paste

HOW TO DO IT
Select a sheet of paper to represent each room in the house. At the top of each page draw a symbol for that room, such as a bed for the bedroom, a table and chairs for the kitchen, and a couch for the living room. Write the name of the room at the top of the page. Talk about the symbols to be sure your child understands them.

Ask your child to find items in the magazines that go into each room. Then sort and paste the items for each room on the appropriate page with the symbol and name at the top.

Cut out a few extra pictures. Ask your child to identify the object in the picture and tell where it goes in the house. Talk about furniture items that could be used in several places.

ANOTHER IDEA
Cut out magazine pictures of objects used in other places such as a store, a library, and a garage.

 Children enjoy this activity because it is like a treasure hunt to find the things that belong in certain places. Besides providing a pleasurable time together, the activity teaches organization skills.

30 PROBLEM SOLVING: Sink or Float

• *Developmental Theme: Reach Out and Explore*

WHY DO IT

This activity helps children practice the problem solving work of science. Making guesses (hypotheses) and checking them are important skills for school and life.

MATERIALS

Objects that float: plastic containers, combs, and bathtub toys
Objects that sink: metal spoons, coins, small stones
Paper/pencil

HOW TO DO IT

Before bath time, place the collected objects near the tub. If a tub is not convenient, use the kitchen or bathroom sink. Ask your child to guess which objects will sink and which objects will float. Have your child test each guess by placing the objects, one at a time, in the water.

Ask your child to sort the objects into two groups: those that float and those that sink. Ask "Why do you think some things float and others do not?"

ANOTHER IDEA

Ask your child to collect small objects to test if they sink or float. After testing each object, help him make a chart with two columns: things that float and things that sink.

 Helping children make choices between alternatives is an important practical everyday skill.

31 *PROBLEM SOLVING: What's Growing?*
Helping children understand reasons why

• *Developmental Theme: Think and Organize*

Have your child plant seeds in two separate cups of soil. Put both cups in a sunny window. Water the soil until the plants start to come up.

Talk with your child about different ways to treat the growing plants. You can move one plant away from the window while the other stays in the sun. You can cover one plant and not the other. Or, you can water one plant, but not the second one.

After a week or two, compare the plants. Ask your child, "How are the plants the same? How are they different? Why do you think one is getting taller and the other is not?" This activity helps children think about cause and effect.

32 *PROBLEM SOLVING: Play It Again*
Helping children help themselves

• *Developmental Theme: Promote Good Daily Habits*

Let your child do her own daily routines as much as possible: select clothing, get dressed, wash up, and brush teeth. Give cues as needed.

This activity helps to perfect the skills of dressing and other basic routines.

When your child wants to repeat an activity, encourage her to do so. Examples would be learning to tie shoes or button clothes. Repetition helps to make a skill automatic.

33 FOCUS: Letter? Color? Number?

• *Developmental Theme: Pre-Read and Respond*

WHY DO IT

This activity helps your child practice working with letters of the alphabet, names of colors, and numbers.

MATERIALS

Heavy paper
Crayons
Scissors
Envelopes to put the papers inside

HOW TO DO IT

Cut the paper into squares and write one letter on each. Lay the squares face down. Have your child pick one and name the letter. When each letter is named correctly, add one new letter and shuffle the squares. Work with your child to name all the letters.

Using crayons, ask your child to color five squares, one color to a square. Write the name of the color on each one. Ask your child to name the color on the square and look at the word. Turn the squares over and have your child select one and name the color. Repeat the action with each square until your child can name the five colors.

ANOTHER IDEA

Use the squares and write one number on each, one to five. Repeat the same process used above until your child can name the five numbers or more correctly.

 Children learn best when they feel secure and experience success. There is no age limit to the need for a positive self-image. By doing these activities you are giving your child the opportunity to be challenged with meaningful work.

34 *FOCUS: The Working World*
Helping child read pictures

• *Developmental Theme: Pre-Read and Respond*

Reading pictures for details helps your child strengthen his ability to understand what is written. Children read in an informal way through pictures. Observing and understanding details increases your child's reading skills.

Look for pictures in magazines and newspapers that have details. Ask your child to answer questions about what he sees in the pictures. For example, "What is happening?" "Who do you see?" "What are they doing?" "What do you think is going to happen next?"

35 *FOCUS: What Do You Like Best?*
Helping children understand their preferences

• *Developmental Theme: Create and Imagine*

In this activity, children have a chance to examine their choices and preferences.

Talk with your child about choices. For example, show your child two colors. Ask which one they prefer. Show your child two foods and ask which one to eat first. Talk about two ice cream flavors and ask your child to choose.

Name two people that your child likes very much. Ask why your child likes them. Ask your child to name a friend and tell why that person is a friend. Help your child name qualities that make a good friend.

36 *RESPECT: When Accidents Happen*
Helping children know what to do

• *Developmental Theme: Promote Good Daily Habits*

When your preschooler spills milk on the floor, explain that you understand that accidents do happen. When she drops something she is carrying and it accidentally breaks, try not to get angry. Instead, ask your child to get a sponge or dishcloth and wipe up the spills or get a broom and dustpan and sweep the floor.

When there is a consistent response to accidents in your home, your child grows up knowing that she is responsible for what she does and that she can handle the consequences.

37 *RESPECT: What's Mine? What's Yours?*

• *Developmental Theme: Connect with Others*

WHY DO IT

This activity helps children to learn to respect other people's privacy.

HOW TO DO IT

Children are curious about and want to play with adult things. Help your child learn the concept of privacy by explaining that some things are not for sharing. For example, "You can't play with mother's special necklace. It is hers." Set aside an off-limits area for a young child.

If your child gets into another family member's things ask, "How do you think that makes people feel?" Let your child draw a happy or sad face to show how people feel.

ANOTHER IDEA

Protect another family member's personal space by closing a door or even locking it if you have to. Enforce this rule so your child knows that you mean it.

 Respect in daily life is shown in many ways: Being dependable and loyal to family and friends, avoiding the temptation to lie or cheat, being fair and honest when playing games, and not disturbing other family members.

38　RESPECT: Praise Others

Helping children learn to give and receive praise

• Developmental Theme: Personal Competency

Gather the family and have each member draw a self-portrait. Label each picture with the family member's name. Attach the pictures to a wall or bulletin board.

Talk with your child about what each picture shows. Have your child say something nice about each person. With your help, write it on the picture. Examples might include: "I like football, too. It's fun having a younger sister. We both love the dog. I'm glad to know you like ice cream."

Ask family members to add compliments to each picture. Keep these pictures posted until everyone has collected a page of praise from others.

39　RESPECT: Remembering What We Do

Helping children remember daily activities

• Developmental Theme: Promote Good Daily Habits

Have your child select an action figure or doll from the toy box. Talk about what daily activities are necessary for the toy and for your child to have a good day.

Let your child pretend to wash, feed, dress, and undress the figure. Talk about other things that occur throughout the day like reading, getting ready for bed, doing chores, playing games, etc.

Children learn words best when using concrete examples. Talking about the actions that happen each day helps your child develop the concepts and language for doing needed daily activities.

41 Activities

8

Taking Big Steps: Ages 4–5 Years

"If you want your children to be brilliant, read them fairy tales. If you want your children to be geniuses, read them more fairy tales."
—Albert Einstein

ACTIVITY   DEVELOPMENTAL THEME

My Place in the Family. . . . . Think and Organize
Telephone Time . . . . Think and Organize
Time Marches On. . . . . Think and Organize

Comic Strip Writing . . . . Create and Imagine
Fitness Counts . . . . Promote Good Daily Habits
People Messages. . . . . Connect with Others
We Want to Know. . . . . Connect with Others

Become a Cooking Wizard. . . . . . . Listen, Speak, and Do
Watch and Learn . . . . Connect with Others
Telling It Together . . . . Create and Imagine

Claim Your Chores. . . . . Promote Good Daily Habits
Stitch and Fix. . . . . Reach Out and Explore
My Place . . . . Think and Organize

Rainy Day . . . . Think and Organize
Field Day. . . . . Reach Out and Explore
Word Entertainment . . . . Pre-Read and Respond

Handling Happenings . . . . Personal Competency
Looking Good . . . . Promote Good Daily Habits
Refine the Reading . . . . Pre-Read and Respond

Applause For My Family . . . . Connect with Others
What Was I Like? . . . . Listen, Speak, and Do
Saying How I Feel . . . . Connect with Others
Family Roots . . . . Create and Imagine

• Welcome to Taking Big Steps

Children four to five years old are asking more and more questions, ever curious. Your child is developing more competencies, handling so much more. Children's memories are sharp. They seem to see everything and eagerly want to tell you about it.

Your child likes choices and is able to make them, such as what to wear, what to eat, and where to go. Keep choices limited so that both of you can live with them.

Children know a lot more about themselves, their families, and where people live. There is a greater feeling of self-control and independence. Look together at family pictures and identify who's who and how you are all related.

Continue your reading. With your help, your child is able to create a book. Staple a few sheets of paper together. Your child makes up a story, dictates it to you, and puts in drawings. Read it together.

Children can sort and classify and use these abilities to help you set the table. They love arts and crafts and are able to make puppets and pictures that tell a story. Talk about feelings, yours and others. This builds empathy and a growing ability to work with and share with others.

Try the activities you find in this chapter. They are all about Learning and Loving.

1 CONFIDENCE: My Place in the Family

• *Developmental Theme: Think and Organize*

WHY DO IT
This activity builds pride and recognizes children's interests.

MATERIALS
Markers
Paste
Large paper
Magazine pictures
Scissors
Snapshots

HOW TO DO IT
The goal is to make a "me" poster. Look through magazines and snapshots with your child. Find pictures of what your child likes—pets, foods, clothes, etc. Together, cut them out and paste them onto a large sheet of paper.

Write sentences on the poster, such as: "Look at me when I was two years old!" "See the picture of my mother." "Look at the fish we caught."

Hang the poster for all to see and enjoy. This activity says to your child, "You are special, and your family knows it."

ANOTHER IDEA
You may want to make poster stories for other family members. Draw pictures of the family and display these around the house.

 Help your child feel and be successful. Provide jobs and activities your child will succeed in and will feel proud of having accomplished. Examples are teaching the family a favorite game, learning to swim, or playing softball.

2   CONFIDENCE: Telephone Time

• Developmental Theme: Think and Organize

WHY DO IT

This activity teaches your child his home telephone number and helps him use number skills.

MATERIALS

Telephone
Small squares of paper
Crayon or pencil

HOW TO DO IT

Show your child his home phone number. Say each number aloud as you point to it.

On separate pieces of paper, write down each number. Show your child how to put the numbered pieces in order to form his phone number. Ask him to read aloud the numbers from the papers. Provide help as needed.

ANOTHER IDEA

As a game, mix up the numbered paper pieces and ask your child to put his phone number in order. Then ask him to write the phone number on a larger piece of paper. Post this paper for other family members to see.

 With your child, develop a personal Telephone Directory. In it, list numbers of friends and family members. Your child can look up and use these numbers.

3 CONFIDENCE: Time Marches On

• *Developmental Theme: Think and Organize*

WHY DO IT

This activity helps your child see and feel the difference between "a few seconds" and "a few minutes." It will help your child learn to be on time.

MATERIALS

Paper
Pencil
A timer, clock or watch with numbers and a second hand

HOW TO DO IT

Make guesses about how long a traffic light is red or green. Then check your guesses using a watch or timer. Make guesses about how long it takes to eat dinner. Then check your guesses.

How long does it take to get ready to go out? How close did each of you come to the right answer?

ANOTHER IDEA

Copy the face of a clock on a cardboard plate. Cut hands out of paper. Attach the hands to the plate and use this to name different times of the day.

 Ask your child to choose a favorite time of day. Together, move the hands to that time. Write a sentence for your child at the bottom of the clock that says "My favorite time of day is _____ because _____."

4 *MOTIVATION: Comic Strip Writing*

Helping children share thoughts

• *Developmental Theme: Create and Imagine*

Use comic strips to help with writing. Cut apart segments of a comic strip and ask your child to arrange them in order.

Choose a comic strip without words. Ask your child to fill in the words of the characters (orally or in writing).

Encourage your child to think of a short story and tell it to you. Ask your child to draw the story in pictures and create an original comic strip. Place a balloon above each character and ask your child to tell you what the character is saying. (You can fill in the small writing.) Post this original comic strip for all to see and enjoy.

5 MOTIVATION: Fitness Counts

• *Developmental Theme: Promote Good Daily Habits*

WHY DO IT

This activity combines learning and practice in a variety of physical and number skills.

MATERIALS

List of simple exercises (touch your toes, jump in place, stretch your arms as high as you can, etc.)
Tape measure
Paper
Pen or pencil
Timer

HOW TO DO IT

Explain a series of simple exercises to your child and try one each day over a period of a few weeks. When you start, use a tape measure to measure each other's height and waist size. Keep track of changes as your exercise plan continues.

Each day increase the number and length of time for doing the exercises.

Use the timer to record how long you can run in place.

ANOTHER IDEA

Use a bathroom scale and have your child weigh herself. Other family members can also get weighed. Children enjoy keeping track of who weighs more and less.

 Eating nutritious snacks is vital for good health. Reserve a small part of your refrigerator for nutritious snack foods such as cut-up fruits and vegetables. This way, there's less risk of your child eating junk foods.

6   MOTIVATION: *People Messages*
Thinking of others

• Developmental Theme: Connect with Others

Together with your child, decide who will get a greeting card. Does a neighbor need cheering up? Is a family member having a birthday? Do you want to thank someone for being especially nice?

Children are great card-makers. First, have your child put a design on the cover. Then, he can find some scraps of paper or materials and glue them on.

Now create a message to go inside the card. For younger children, you write the message as they dictate it to you. The message can be as short as, "I love you!" Or it can be a longer note such as "Have a Happy Birthday and many more!"

Help your child address the card and put it in the mail.

7   MOTIVATION: *We Want to Know*
Asking questions to learn about each other

• Developmental Theme: Connect with Others

With your child, list several easy questions for both of you to answer. Sample questions might be: What is your favorite color? dessert? place to go? sport? TV program? List each question separately. Leave room on the page for your child to fill in answers with you.

When friends come to visit, ask them to let your child interview them and write their answers. Help as needed. This is a record of what your family and visitors like. It is interesting to review this with your child. You will learn things about family and friends you probably didn't know.

8 *EFFORT: Become a Cooking Wizard*
Helping children follow recipes

• *Developmental Theme: Listen, Speak, and Do*

Following a recipe and making measurements uses beginning math and reading skills. Find simple recipes in newspapers and magazines that you can try with your child.

Read the directions aloud to your child. With your child, practice measuring and following directions together. This is what we do first, second, and so on.

Start a recipe collection of foods that you cook together. Working closely with your child and making something together builds positive family relationships.

9 *EFFORT: Watch and Learn*
Helping children recognize hard work

• *Developmental Theme: Connect with Others*

A child's effort remains strong when parents share in the excitement about new discoveries and new skills.

Take your child to places where she can watch people at work—a construction site, a grocery store, the post office, an office. Talk about what the people are doing, what tools they use, how they are dressed, whether they seem to enjoy their work.

Point out effort when you see it—a helpful grocery store clerk, the traffic guard at the corner, the ticket taker at the movie.

As children get older, knowing about effort helps them continue to keep learning.

10 EFFORT: *Telling It Together*

Practicing language and creativity to prepare for reading

• *Developmental Theme: Create and Imagine*

Explain to your child that this activity is about taking turns telling a story that you make up together.

Decide upon a topic. Any will do—for example, my best friend, my favorite store, TV, fairy tales, even the weather. You might begin with "Once upon a time…"

Take turns adding to the story by developing the characters, setting, and story line. The story ends when you both agree it is finished, perhaps after ten sentences.

It can be a silly story, but it must have a beginning, a middle, and an end. This gives children a sense of start-to-finish. It takes effort.

11 *RESPONSIBILITY: Claim Your Chores*

• *Developmental Theme: Promote Good Daily Habits*

WHY DO IT
Set aside time to teach your child how to do basic chores.

HOW TO DO IT
Make a list of the chores to be done. Young children can learn to sort clean laundry into piles for different family members, pick out clothes for the next day, dust and vacuum, clear the table after meals, and put items in the sink or dishwasher.

Ask your child: What jobs are you doing now? Which ones would you like to do?

ANOTHER IDEA
Try a Chore Chart such as this one:

Task   Day

_____   _____

_____   _____

 Check off the chores as they are finished. Children may want to switch jobs once a week. Making a contribution to help the house run smoothly is a worthy goal.

12 RESPONSIBILITY: Stitch and Fix
Helping build self-reliance

• *Developmental Theme: Reach Out and Explore*

The next time your child loses a button from a shirt, ask if he would like to learn how to sew the button back on. If you don't have the missing button, look for one of similar size and color. Next, select a needle with a large eye and some thread that matches the clothing.

Show your child how to thread the needle and tie a knot in the end. Sit next to your child to keep him safe. Then, step-by-step, together sew on the button.

You can practice sewing even when a button doesn't need to be sewn. Get a piece of fabric, some buttons, needle, and thread and ask your child to practice. You can cut the buttons off and repeat this activity until children perfect the skill.

13 RESPONSIBILITY: My Place

• Developmental Theme: Think and Organize

WHY DO IT

This activity helps family members keep track of personal items used at school and on the job. It cuts down on family morning stress.

MATERIALS

Cardboard boxes for every family member

For decorating the boxes: magazines; paper; artwork; markers; wrapping paper; glue; scissors; ruler

HOW TO DO IT

Have your child decorate the boxes with pictures, words, or artwork. For practice in math, your child can use the ruler to measure the boxes.

Place the boxes in a convenient spot where your child can drop school things, such as a notebook, and parents can drop job things, such as glasses and gloves. When child and parent come home, the boxes should be the first stop. Then, everything is in one place for the next day.

ANOTHER IDEA

Set up a box for your child's special "little treasures." Put in special activities, workbooks, games, or books.

 Reward your child for using her boxes. Leave brief notes or drawings in the box congratulating your child for getting organized.

14 *INITIATIVE: Rainy Day Fun*
Creating fun and learning on bad weather days

• *Developmental Theme: Think and Organize*

Set up a rainy day box. Fill it with workbooks, games, books, a new pencil or marker, paper, scissors, and glue.

Set up a special study corner your child can use for quiet activities and give your child the box to put items inside. Help your child decorate the box and study area. Hang pictures and your child's artwork on the wall.

Show your pleasure when your child uses the rainy day box regularly. Leave special notes to praise your child for keeping items in order. Invite other members of the family to put surprises in the box.

This activity helps children get organized. It cuts down on last-minute panic in trying to find things when timelines are short.

15 *INITIATIVE: Field Day*

• *Developmental Theme: Reach Out and Explore*

WHY DO IT

This activity builds motor skills, including balance, spatial awareness, agility, and strength.

MATERIALS

Hula hoops
Boxes
Colored chalk or cardboard
Watch or clock

HOW TO DO IT

Use the hoops to create a jumping game. Place the hoops on the ground and invite your child to jump or hop through each hoop forward, sideways, and backward.

Set up an obstacle course by using boxes of different sizes for your child to walk around or crawl through. Set this up near a slide or swing set. Your child can finish the obstacle course by climbing the ladder, swinging, or sliding down the slide.

Your child can make stop signs or use chalk to draw signs on the ground for traffic signals.

ANOTHER IDEA

Use a watch to time your child as he goes through the obstacle course. Time several trials and see if he gets faster with practice.

 Encourage your child to make up his own games. This builds creativity. Ask your child to create a new game using the hoops or the boxes. Join in by inventing a new game yourself.

16 INITIATIVE: Word Entertainment

• *Developmental Theme: Pre-Read and Respond*

WHY DO IT
This activity increases your child's vocabulary using a daily game activity.

MATERIALS
Paper
Marker
Small Box

HOW TO DO IT
Each day, post a new word in your child's room and discuss the meaning of the word.

Decorate a small box for the new words and review them once a week. Ask children what words they would like to know and spell. Write these and post for your child to see. After your child knows these, put them into the "word box."

ANOTHER IDEA
Have a theme week where all the new words are in the same category, like color words, transportation words, outdoor words, kitchen words, and so on.

Academic success is very dependent upon the size of your child's vocabulary. Word activities and games contribute to your child's level of literacy. Encourage your child to suggest words for you to use in sentences.

17 PERSEVERANCE: *Handling Happenings*
Extending your child's attention span

• *Developmental Theme: Personal Competency*

Help your child understand perseverance by talking about a real experience that required you or your child to wait or took extra time to finish. Perhaps your child had to grow a plant before its flowers bloomed. Or there was a long line at the bank, the car wash, or the grocery store.

Talk with your child about having something to do for the times while you are waiting. This might include reading a picture book or drawing.

Was there ever a time when you had to finish something even though you were tired? Share stories with your child about patience and the need to keep on trying.

18 PERSEVERANCE: *Looking Good*
Helping children do more for themselves

• *Developmental Theme: Promote Good Daily Habits*

Children need to be able to take care of their own personal grooming with less nagging from parents.

Create a chart that lists grooming activities and post it next to the sink. Draw a box next to each activity so your child can put a check in it after the activity is complete. Attach a crayon with a string to the chart. Read the chart aloud to your child.

Include activities such as:
- I brushed my teeth.
- I washed my face.
- I washed my hands.
- I combed my hair.

19 PERSEVERANCE: Refine the Reading
Forming positive reading habits

• *Developmental Theme: Pre-Read and Respond*

Set aside a time each day (ten to fifteen minutes) when the family reads. The rule is that everyone must choose a book or something else to read.

Give a baby or young toddler a clean, cuddly, cloth book to handle and chew on during this time. An older child can choose to look at a picture book or review a favorite storybook.

Create a relaxed atmosphere. Put oversized pillows on the floor for extra reading space.

Let nothing interfere with your reading time together. If you have guests present during family reading time, invite them to read too.

20 CARING: Applause for My Family

• *Developmental Theme: Connect with Others*

WHY DO IT
This activity spotlights the special qualities of every person and encourages positive behavior.

MATERIALS
Pen or pencil
Paper

HOW TO DO IT
With your child, think about each family member and write the positive qualities, abilities, and talents of this person. Ask your child to contribute. Some examples:

_____ helped me when I couldn't reach the top shelf in closet.
_____ told me I did a good job at cleaning up
_____ took special time to read to me.

Brainstorm positive ideas for each family member. Post the lists for all to see.

ANOTHER IDEA
Ask family members to write a list of their own positive qualities. Read the list and ask your child to guess who the person is.

 Recognizing and supporting positive qualities in others develops good habits that last well beyond these activities.

21 *CARING: What Was I Like?*
Helping children understand family relationships

• *Developmental Theme: Listen, Speak, and Do*

Talk with your child about her infancy. Children like to hear about themselves. They feel more capable now when you talk about how helpless they used to be.

Tell stories about events that took place in your child's life: "The Day You Took Your First Step" or "When You Learned to Go Down the Slide by Yourself." Ask your child to tell you what she remembers.

Show pictures of yourself when you were the age of your child. Children love to hear stories of your own growing up.

22 *CARING: Saying How I Feel*
Helping children understand their feelings

• *Developmental Theme: Connect with Others*

Talk to your child about feelings—his own, yours, those of other family members or a friend at school. Some questions to ask include: "How do you think I feel when you give me a hug?" "How did you feel when you fell down?" "What does it feel like when a friend will not play with you?" "How do you think Grandma feels when we come to visit her?"

Ask your child to show you with body language how he feels at different times. For example, going on vacation, catching a fish, having a special time with you, getting new shoes, or talking with a friend.

You can ask your child to draw pictures about feelings and then talk about them: "Tell me about your drawing."

23 CARING: *Family Roots*
Helping build a sense of family pride

• *Developmental Theme: Create and Imagine*

Select a group of family photographs and talk with your child about the people you see and what they are doing. Ask your child to choose several pictures for a personal family album. Try to include pictures of even the youngest members of the family.

Attach the pictures to paper, one to a page. Ask your child to dictate a few sentences and a title for each picture. Fasten the pages together to form a small book. Make a title and decorate the cover. Number the pages. Add to the album over time as your family grows and changes.

24 TEAMWORK: Putting Words Together

• *Developmental Theme: Pre-Read and Respond*

WHY DO IT

Teamwork is an important skill to develop. In this activity your child builds language skills and practices taking turns.

HOW TO DO IT

With your child, make up a story. Decide on a topic and take turns, adding one sentence at a time. The first sentence might begin, "Once upon a time a little girl lived in a magic land."

ANOTHER IDEA

Ask questions to help your child develop the story, characters, setting, and action. Props can help. Use hats and scarves. Soon a character emerges.

 Children improve their language skills by making up stories. They begin to understand how ideas flow from one to another and that everyone's ideas are important.

25 TEAMWORK: Conserving Resources

• *Developmental Theme: Personal Competency*

WHY DO IT
You and your child can work as a team to conserve energy and money.

HOW TO DO IT
Take a home electricity tour. Ask your child to think of ways you use electricity for televisions and radios, for lights, for heat and air conditioning.

Talk about the ways you can conserve electricity. Turn off televisions and radios when they aren't being used. Turn off lights when leaving a room. Adjust the heat and air conditioning at night. Put your energy conservation ideas into action.

ANOTHER IDEA
Brainstorm with your child ways to conserve gasoline. Some ideas are taking fewer trips to the grocery store, accomplishing several errands on one trip, lowering speed on the highway, and sharing rides with others.

 Look at your energy bills over the next few months. Share the bills with your child so she can be proud to be a contributing member of the conservation team.

26 *TEAMWORK: Young Shopper*
Helping children learn smart shopping skills

• *Developmental Theme: Reach Out and Explore*

Making grocery lists provides good practice in reading and writing, and it helps families plan what to buy. It can save money when you are shopping for food, and it minimizes impulse buying.

As you go down each supermarket aisle, ask your child, "Will we find something on our list here?" Your child will be kept busy looking for and finding items.

Let young readers check off items on your list as you put them into the cart.

27 *COMMON SENSE: Food and Money*
Develop a sense of money and how much food costs

• *Developmental Theme: Pre-Read and Respond*

Save the grocery receipt from your shopping trip. As you put away the groceries at home, ask your child to use the receipt to find the items you bought and their prices. As the items are put away, they are checked off the receipt. Your child becomes aware of food the family uses and the cost of these items.

On the next trip to the grocery store, have your child pick out one item within a price limit you set. Your child will like making this choice.

You can expand this activity by saving clean food cans and empty boxes to set up a "Home Store." Use play money, too.

28 *COMMON SENSE: String Along Sentences*
Helping children improve language skills

• *Developmental Theme: Pre-Read and Respond*

Good writers know how to string words together in an interesting way. Ask your child for an idea or name of something. Write several of these words down on a large piece of paper.

With your child, make a sentence with the words. For example, the words may be CAT, POPCORN, EATING, and ROSE. You might put these together like this: "I saw a fat cat with a rose in his paw standing and eating popcorn."

The sillier the sentence, the more laughs you will have—and the stronger your child will become in using a variety of words and sentences.

29 COMMON SENSE: Safe Is Smart

• *Developmental Theme: Personal Competency*

WHY DO IT

Talk with your child about safety and how to behave in an emergency.

MATERIALS

Pen or Pencil
Paper

HOW TO DO IT

Discuss the importance of being cautious without making your child too fearful. Talk about what to do if someone your child does not know asks him to get in a car or come with them. Practice the actions and behaviors you expect your child to do in these situations. Role-play the parts. Exchange roles and do the situation again.

Talk with your child about how to act in an emergency such as getting hurt, being scared, or losing the key to the house. Together develop steps to take in emergency situations. Write the steps so they can be reviewed.

ANOTHER IDEA

Take a walk in your neighborhood. Together with your child, point out objects or areas that are unsafe. Explain that knowing what to do in an emergency can make a big difference in staying safe.

 As you talk with your child about safety and how to behave in an emergency, you will become more aware of what you can do as a parent to create a safer environment for your family.

30 *PROBLEM SOLVING: Fire! It's an Emergency*
Helping children keep safe

• *Developmental Theme: Personal Competency*

To prepare for a fire emergency, walk through your house with your child and point out possible exits. Explain the safe way to exit.

Remind your child that if there is a lot of smoke, she needs to crawl on her hands and knees close to the floor to get to an exit. Create a plan for all family members to meet together outside. Hold practice fire drills with the family.

Having a plan before an emergency is a smart thing to do. Children will observe that thinking and planning ahead makes an emergency less frightening.

See page 203 for a related activity, "Know, Choose, and Succeed."

31 PROBLEM SOLVING: What Do We Think?

• *Developmental Theme: Think and Organize*

WHY DO IT
This activity gives young children practice in asking questions and making small decisions before they have to make big ones.

HOW TO DO IT
Ask your child to pretend one of the following events has happened:

  • He drops a glass of milk on the floor.
  • Two different friends ask to play with him at the same time.
  • He gets lost in the supermarket.

Ask your child to think of as many ways as possible to solve these problems. Let your child pick the solution that seems the best and tell why.

ANOTHER IDEA
Before stepping in to solve a problem, encourage your child's problem solving abilities by first asking, "What do you think?"

When a child's first solution doesn't work, parents can say, "What else might work?" Children become experts at problem solving when they ask and answer lots of questions.

32 PROBLEM SOLVING: What's Your Opinion?
Encouraging children to think

• *Developmental Theme: Personal Competency*

Ask your child thoughtful, open-ended questions that have no right or wrong answers. Encourage your child to think about the answers and give an opinion.

Avoid questions that have one correct answer, such as "What color is…" or "How old are you?"

Ask open-ended questions, such as:

- What do you think about…?
- What might happen if…?
- How could we fix this broken…?
- What do you think will happen next in this story?

To help you get into the habit of asking open-ended questions, you can write some questions on a piece of paper and post them. Children of all ages benefit when they are asked to offer their ideas and opinions.

33 PROBLEM SOLVING: Rhyme Time
Helping children hear and say rhyming words

• *Developmental Theme: Listen, Speak, and Do*

Make a list of everyday household words that have rhyming matches. For example: bed and head, floor and door, hat and cat, dog and log, etc.

Write each word on a piece of paper. Write one letter on other pieces. Use consonants that start words such as B, C, D, L, M, and P. Make two paper piles.

Ask your child to pick one piece of paper from each pile. See if a rhyming word is possible. Your child might pick "look" and the letter B to make "book." Say it aloud. Sometimes a real word is not possible. So try a make-believe word. This game makes learning even more fun.

34 FOCUS: Counting Minutes

• *Developmental Theme: Listen, Speak, and Do*

WHY DO IT

This activity helps your child get ready for studying science by becoming a keen observer.

MATERIALS

Paper
Pencil
Clock or watch with a second hand

HOW TO DO IT

Ask your child to watch the second hand tick five seconds. Count the seconds together. Ask your child, "Was that a long or short time?"

Then count off thirty seconds together. Check to see how many times your child can clap hands during this time. Trade places and have your child count your clapping.

Go outside. Ask your child to walk with you for one minute. Count your steps as you walk together.

ANOTHER IDEA

Time other activities, such as jumping. Ask your child to jump for ten seconds. Ask your child to tell you when she thinks ten seconds have passed.

 Having a sense of how long a task takes is an important skill in everyday living. Being able to follow directions and guess when you will be finished also helps your child use estimation skills.

35 FOCUS: Wholesome Choices
Helping children eat well

• Developmental Theme: Practice Good Daily Habits

Children feel close to parents who listen to and use their ideas. Try this for food shopping. As you plan your shopping trip together, your child chooses a food from each of the main food groups: vegetables, fruits, meats, dairy products, and grains.

To begin, your child might choose one bread product, one dairy product, and one fruit. Write your child's choices on your shopping list. At the store, let your child find these items.

36 FOCUS: Let's Exchange
Remembering children who are away

• Developmental Theme: Reach Out and Explore

Today many families are blended, with children who are half-sisters and half-brothers. Children may live with one parent and come for brief visits to be with the other parent. It is sometimes sad for visiting children to leave siblings and return to their "other" house.

Here's one activity that can help. With your child, find and decorate special boxes that can be left behind. Before your child ends the visit, have him select something special to leave behind for the family when he is gone. This can be a special necklace, small toy, special note, stuffed animal, etc. Each member of the family finds one thing or writes a note for the visiting child to find next time in the special box.

37 FOCUS: My Favorite Car

• *Developmental Theme: Think and Organize*

WHY DO IT

When children develop their abilities to distinguish color, shape, and size, they are assembling language skills needed for reading.

HOW TO DO IT

Find a seat (inside or outside) that allows you and your child to see automobiles as they park or pass by on the street. Ask your child to point out or name a favorite car. Encourage your child to tell why that car is special.

ANOTHER IDEA

Ask your child to pick a color such as blue and find blue cars parked on the street or passing by. Add new colors next time.

 Continue this game on a fairly regular basis, using more and more language each time. Use other categories to identify the child's favorite sports, movies, TV characters, and computer games.

38 RESPECT: Saying It Nicely
Helping children express positive feelings toward others

• Developmental Theme: Connect with Others

Make it a family ritual to end each day by saying something nice about each other. You might tell your child, "I liked the way you helped your brother find his lost shoe" or "I noticed that you got ready for bed the first time I asked." Your child might say to a sibling, "I liked it when you shared your cookie."

Older children may write their notes. Younger children can dictate their messages. Whether spoken or written, these messages will help children express their positive feelings and learn how it feels when someone tells them something nice.

39 RESPECT: Lucky Us
Saying what's good about each other

• Developmental Theme: Connect with Others

Decorate a jar or small box with colored paper. Write "Lucky Us" on the outside. Once a week have each family member write one positive sentence about another member of the family. Place the slips into the jar.

When writing these sentences, help your child focus on special abilities. Ask questions such as: What is special about you? What is special about your brother or sister? What is special about mommy, daddy, grandmother, grandfather?

At the end of the month, open the jar or box and read what each person has written. There will be joy for everyone as there are only positive things to be shared.

40 RESPECT: I Believe It Means...
Defining important words

• *Developmental Theme: Listen, Speak, and Do*

Ask your child what "respect" means. Share what the word means to you. Does your child mention that we treat others as we want others to act toward us?

Make a list of words that are connected to respect, words such as honor, appreciation, praise, value, and consideration.

Help your child to think of times when respect was shown toward others. Examples might be when your child borrowed something and returned it in good condition or helped a family member get a job done more quickly.

41 RESPECT: Reasoning with Children
Helping children understand rules

• *Developmental Theme: Connect with Others*

Each family's rules may be different from their neighbor's. Arguing with your child about whose rules are best can cause friction. Good rules have sound reasons to back them up.

Children will break rules to be sure they are still in effect. At different ages, a child might test rules by tantrums or disobedience.

Talk with your child about your family's rules. Allow your child to present a case to change a rule—without a battle. You won't lose face by changing the rule when your child has convinced you with a persuasive argument. This will help your child work with rules. By doing this activity, your child will learn a lesson in self-respect and respect for you, too.

42 Activities

9

*Opening
School Doors:
Ages 5–6 Years*

"If we don't stand up
for our children, then
we don't stand
for much!"
-Marion Wright Edelman

ACTIVITY	DEVELOPMENTAL THEME
The "Good Night" Formula	Listen, Speak, and Do
Our Family Tree	Connect with Others
Doing It All	Promote Good Daily Habits
Numbers Galore	Pre-Read and Respond
Market Sense	Pre-Read and Respond
How Much Time?	Personal Competency
Prepare and Plan	Personal Competency
I Know, I Know	Personal Competency
Gather That Information	Pre-Read and Respond
From Start to Finish	Personal Competency
Promise! Promise!	Personal Competency
Money Matters	Personal Competency
A Perfect Smile	Promote Good Daily Habits
Weigh Me	Promote Good Daily Habits
Snug, Secure, and Safe	Promote Good Daily Habits
What's Inside?	Reach Out and Explore
Letter to My Teacher	Reach Out and Explore
Timeless Tasks	Think and Organize
Coupon Hunt	Pre-Read and Respond
Getting It Done	Promote Good Daily Habits
Signaling for Help	Personal Competency
Interview Magic	Create and Imagine
Those Who Help	Connect with Others
What's Important to You?	Create and Imagine

• *Opening School Doors*

Knowing the alphabet and counting to ten are nice things to know before school. Yet they are not the foundation on which school success rests. Here are the real ABCs:

A. How are my child's social and group skills? How can I help my child learn to take turns, sit down, pay attention, and respect the rights of others?

B. How are my child's organizing skills? What can I do to help my child work in an orderly, systematic way?

C. How does my child react to situations personally? How can I help my child handle disappointment, tolerate frustration, and get his/her own needs met, even in a large group?

Our children need to build these abilities and hear these messages of encouragement from us:

- Things happen.
- They don't kill us.
- There is always another day.
- Have courage.
- Remember, we love you.

Try the activities in this chapter. They are all about Learning and Loving.

1 ## CONFIDENCE: The "Good Night" Formula
Helping children think positive thoughts

• Developmental Theme: Listen, Speak, and Do

Just before you say "good night" to your child, share a few private moments together. Take turns asking each other some of the following questions:

- What is one thing you like or love about me?
- What is one good thing that happened during the day?
- What is one thing you are looking forward to tomorrow?
- What is a wish, a hope, a dream, or a goal that you have?

This activity builds a feeling of closeness just before your child goes to sleep.

2 ## CONFIDENCE: Our Family Tree
Helping children learn about their family history

• Developmental Theme: Connect with Others

Together, draw the outline of a tree with branches on a large piece of paper or paper bag.

Place your family's last name in large letters on the trunk of the tree and your child's name at the top of the tree. Fill in as many branches of the tree as you can with family names and relationships. Share stories about family members. Encourage your child to ask questions.

Talk with your child about your family tree, what you did when you were young, where you lived, who you played with, what your brothers and sisters were like. Share family snapshots. Your child will enjoy hearing about everyone.

This activity can last several sessions, especially when you have conversations about other relatives. Save the family tree paper, decorate and post it for all family members to enjoy.

3 *CONFIDENCE: Doing It All*

• *Developmental Theme: Promote Good Daily Habits*

WHY DO IT

This activity helps children use after school time wisely.

MATERIALS

Pen or pencil
Paper

HOW TO DO IT

Make a list with your child of the tasks that are done at home. Count the number of hours your child has from the time she gets home from school until bedtime. Together, plan a weekly schedule for this after-school time. Here's an example:

Day	Homework	Chores	Sports/Hobbies	Computer/TV
Monday				
Tuesday				
Etc.				

Write and post this weekly schedule and see how it is working. It takes time to get into the swing of keeping track of time. Once you get into the habit, you wonder how you got along without doing it before.

ANOTHER IDEA

Talk about what you would do if there were an extra hour in every day. What do you enjoy most? Least? Think of this as a "delicious" hour and be creative in your thinking.

 Help your child make a list of the things to remember to do on one specific day. Leave enough time to complete each task. When a task gets done, use a marker and cross off that item. At the end of the day, it is satisfying to see a list on which everything is marked, "Done."

4 CONFIDENCE: Numbers Galore

• *Developmental Theme: Pre-Read and Respond*

WHY DO IT

This activity teaches children to recognize that numbers are used on many objects. Being able to read these numbers helps children feel confident about numbers and math.

MATERIALS

Magazines, newspapers, and mail advertisements that show numbers
Paper
Scissors
Paste/glue
Marker

HOW TO DO IT

Take a trip through the house. Ask your child where numbers are found and how they are used. Look for objects such as clocks, pages in books, electric meters, the dials of washers and dryers, and the inside of shoes and clothing tags. Look at the labels, telephone, and calendars.

ANOTHER IDEA

On another day look for numbers *outside* the house. Find numbers when traveling in the car or walking around the neighborhood. Look for numbers on the car's speedometer, clock, radio, and license plates. Look on house and street signs, road signs, billboards, and cash register tapes.

 Show your child what large numbers such as one billion look like and talk about what they are named. Look for big numbers that will stretch your child's imagination. Try to find numbers with many zeros in them.

5 *MOTIVATION: Market Sense*
Developing math skills with a practical task

• *Developmental Theme: Pre-Read and Respond*

In the grocery store, when you are not in a hurry to complete the shopping, let your child find the prices of items you place in the cart. If you have a small calculator, teach your child to use it.

Have your child practice entering several prices, using the addition (plus) sign and the total keys. Practice several times until your child feels comfortable and has gained proficiency in entering and totaling numbers.

If you do not have a calculator, have your child call out the price of each item and estimate what the items will cost at check out. Your child can practice adding two items together.

Try the self-checkout line. Call out the prices and help your child scan the items. Check to see how the machine total matches your child's figures. When you do this activity several times, you give your child a chance to be more accurate so the estimate is closer to the actual cost.

6 *MOTIVATION: How Much Time?*
Helping children understand how long activities take

• *Developmental Theme: Personal Competency*

This activity helps your child understand how time flies. For example, read a book together for five minutes. Count how many pages you read. Is your child surprised by how many pages can be read in five minutes?

Have your child time two TV commercials. Compare the results.

Time your child during daily routines such as brushing teeth, getting ready for bed, setting the table, doing homework. Talk about the time used for each activity.

Have your child time you doing computer messages, cooking dinner, opening mail. Then ask your child to report the findings.

7 MOTIVATION: Prepare and Plan
Helping children develop successful study habits

• *Developmental Theme: Personal Competency*

Parents do a lot of organizing for children. Children need to be able to organize themselves in order to fulfill their work in school and go beyond it.

What does it take to do homework efficiently and well? It takes having things ready. It takes knowing what to do first. In the early school years, it takes an easy level of planning. As children grow older, it takes the ability to seek and find information. Here are some basics:

A Quiet Place for Study and Reading. A chair, a table, a lamp, a plant, a small table in a corner of the room. A small lap board for drawing and writing in bed can also encourage good study attitudes.

Books and Magazines Around Us. Children need to see parents reading, and they also need to be read to. Children need to be able to find a book and magazine that they can pick up and read themselves. Reading needs to be part of our daily lives.

8 EFFORT: I Know, I Know
Helping children be prepared in case of emergency

• *Developmental Theme: Personal Competency*

It takes effort to be safe. Prepare a safety kit with your child. Include an identification card with basic facts: name, address, phone number. Additional items may be a picture of your child; list of important numbers; coins for a telephone call, and perhaps an energy bar or small snack.

Review the information and items with your child. Practice saying the identification card facts with the child. Put these safety facts inside a clear plastic bag. Tape it inside your child's lunch box or school bag.

Show your child your own identification card in your wallet. Children will feel very grown-up having their own information card.

9 *EFFORT: Gather That Information*

Helping children use information

• *Developmental Theme: Pre-Read and Respond*

Asking questions is a good way to learn. Have your child call the movie theater to find out the times for a show. How much does a ticket cost? Call the local library to find out the hours that they are open. Plan ahead to visit the local fire station and ask questions of the firefighters.

Have your child share with you how the information gathered can be put to use.

When children feel comfortable asking questions of adults, it supports their wanting to learn more. Children need to know how to ask questions, gather information, and use the results to make decisions.

10 EFFORT: From Start to Finish

• *Developmental Theme: Personal Competency*

WHY DO IT

It is important to organize your thinking and materials to do a job before you begin it. This activity gives practice in beginning and finishing a job.

MATERIALS

Paper
Pencil

HOW TO DO IT

Together, select one job your child usually does around the house, such as setting the table, clearing the dishes, taking out the garbage, or feeding a pet. Ask your child to list the Start, Do, and Finish steps needed for the new job. Write them together. Try out the list and see how it works.

Here's an example for watering plants.
- Start: Get a watering can or another container and some paper towels in case water is spilled.
- Do: Fill the container with lukewarm water. Feel the dirt around the plants to see which plants need water. Water the plants and wipe up spilled water. Pick off dead leaves from the plant.
- Finish: Throw the dead leaves and wet paper towels in the trash container. Put the container away.

ANOTHER IDEA

Add a new job that your child has never done. Ask your child to list the Start, Do, and Finish steps needed for the new job. Write them together. Try out the plan and see how it works.

 Talk about ways to improve getting the job done. Talk about one of the jobs you do around the house. Ask your child to think of ways to improve the steps you use.

11 RESPONSIBILITY: Promise! Promise!

• *Developmental Theme: Personal Competency*

WHY DO IT

This activity helps children become more personally responsible by following through on their promises. It helps children realize what it means to keep promises.

HOW TO DO IT

Talk with your child about what happens when people don't do what they are responsible for doing. For example, plants that don't get watered wilt. Animals and children that don't get fed get hungry. Garbage smells if it isn't taken outside.

Discuss the consequences when tasks are not done. Is it fair to expect others to do our work? Is it responsible?

Decide together on tasks for each family member. Should people be able to do only the things they like? Yes or no? Talk about this.

ANOTHER IDEA

When your child argues with you about assigned tasks, ask him to think about what would happen if parents decided they didn't want to work, shop, or cook meals, or if the school bus driver stayed home. Talk about more examples together.

 Share with your child how using the MegaSkill responsibility as an adult has helped you.

12 RESPONSIBILITY: Money Matters
Helping children learn how to save money

• *Developmental Theme: Personal Competency*

Share with your child examples of the different ways to save money when you shop. These include clipping food coupons, buying larger quantities, comparing prices at different stores, and looking for best buys.

Go to the store. Shop using your money-saving strategies. At home, give your child a pencil and the store receipt to check off the prices of items as you take them out of the bag. With your child, figure out how much money you saved on your shopping trip.

13 *RESPONSIBILITY: A Perfect Smile*

• *Developmental Theme: Promote Good Daily Habits*

WHY DO IT

Teach your child about the proper care of teeth to promote good personal hygiene practices.

MATERIALS

Paper
Pen or pencil

HOW TO DO IT

With your child, write two headings at the top of a piece of paper: "Friends of Teeth" and "Enemies of Teeth." List all the good things you can do for your teeth under Friends of Teeth. Under Enemies of Teeth, include the danger signals of bleeding, swollen gums, a hole in the tooth, sensitivity to hot and/or cold.

Talk about what hurts teeth like hard candy, not brushing at bedtime, using teeth as "bottle openers." Post the chart where children brush their teeth as a reminder of good health habits.

ANOTHER IDEA

Ask questions like, "Can teeth last forever? Why or why not?" "Does a great smile influence the first impression you make with another person?"

 It's easy to neglect teeth because going to the dentist is sometimes not very pleasant. Making this chart with your child prompts you to schedule regular visits to the dentist.

14 INITIATIVE: Weigh Me

• *Developmental Theme: Promote Good Daily Habits*

WHY DO IT

This activity teaches children how to use a scale. Practicing reading and recording numbers in real life helps children work with numbers in school.

MATERIALS

Produce scale
Fruits and vegetables to be weighed
Pencil/pen and paper

HOW TO DO IT

Find a scale that your child can reach and read. Put items on the scale and read the numbers together. A good place to find a scale is in the fruit and vegetable section of the supermarket. Choose a day and time when the store is not too busy.

Look at the numbers on the scale. First find the pound (lb.) and half-pound (1/2 lb.) marks. Then find the quarter-pound (1/4 lb.) mark. Look for other fractions of a pound.

ANOTHER IDEA

Choose three or four produce items to weigh. These items might be potatoes, onions, or fruit. Help your child weigh the items separately and write down the weights. Which weighs the most? Which weighs the least? Take one piece away and see how it changes the weight.

 Have your child choose one piece of fruit, weigh it, and take it home to eat. Learning to use the scale makes numbers more real to your child, and eating fruit is a healthy thing to do.

15 *INITIATIVE: Snug, Secure, and Safe*

• *Developmental Theme: Promote Good Daily Habits*

WHY DO IT

Talking about safety rules in advance prepares your child for emergencies.

HOW TO DO IT

Think about three different places where safety rules are strict. Examples might be at a swimming pool, a sports event, or when driving a car.

From your own experience, make a list of rules you follow for safety in these situations, such as look both ways before crossing the street. Discuss these with your child. What could happen if the rules are not followed?

Talk about how the rules are enforced. Do you and your child have suggestions for changing a rule or enforcing it differently? Talk about these ideas.

ANOTHER IDEA

When people disagree with certain rules, do you think it is all right for them to break the rule? Why or why not? Discuss these questions with your child.

 Rules are made because a change is necessary in the way we are doing things. Help your child to understand that obeying rules helps keep all of us safer and more secure.

16 INITIATIVE: What's Inside?
Sparking a child's curiosity about how things work

• *Developmental Theme: Reach Out and Explore*

For this activity use a machine that is broken and not repairable, such as a small clock, radio, or typewriter. Ask your child if she would like to take it apart to discover how the machine works and what is inside.

The machine should not be plugged in at any time during this activity. Watch out for sharp parts.

Cover a table with newspaper. Put out a few tools and a flashlight to see the inside of the broken machine. Allow your child to do the work of taking the machine apart as you look on. Put the small pieces together in groups. After investigating how the machine works, your child may want to reassemble the machine as it was in the beginning.

Ask your child to think about inventing a new machine. What would it do? How would it work? Who would be interested in using it? What would it cost? Share your ideas.

17 INITIATIVE: Letter to My Teacher
Helping children share interests and goals with others

• *Developmental Theme: Reach Out and Explore*

Talk with your child about what it will be like to begin "real" school. Help your child feel more at ease by suggesting that you write a letter together introducing your child to the teacher. Let your child choose things to share in this letter such as favorite things, toys, foods, hobbies, places to visit, colors, interests, and activities the family does together for fun and learning.

With your child name three goals for the first year of school. Examples might be making new friends, writing my name and address, riding the school bus, reading books, and using the computer.

Make two copies of your child's letter. Try to arrange to visit the school before opening day and deliver the letter to the teacher. Post the other letter for family members to see. Remind your child about the goals. Ask your family to encourage your child's efforts in reaching these goals.

18 *PERSEVERANCE: Timeless Tasks*
Teaching a child to wait for a reward

• *Developmental Theme: Think and Organize*

Involve your child in a task that takes a long time to complete, such as taking care of a vegetable garden, organizing the tool chest, getting ready for a family celebration, or cleaning out the garage.

A lot happens before you can harvest a vegetable garden, for example. Review the steps with your child. Here are some basic steps:

- Preparing the soil
- Planting the seeds
- Weeding, hoeing, staking, and watering
- Watering
- Checking for bugs or picking off dead leaves
- Checking for ripeness
- Harvesting the crop

When the plants finally produce real vegetables, you and your child can both feel proud that you stuck to the task.

See Whose Turn Is It? in this chapter for another version of this activity.

PERSEVERANCE: Coupon Hunt

19 Helping children fill out forms

• *Developmental Theme: Pre-Read and Respond*

Helping your child develop the ability to concentrate on one task to be done is an important skill.

Find coupons in newspapers and magazines. Fill out requests for free items and enter contests. Have your child fill out as much information as possible, address the envelope, and enclose a self-addressed envelope inside, if requested. Review what is needed for the return address. Apply stamps and send for the free material.

Children are excited to receive mail and free items. Requesting information and preparing the forms are academic skills.

20 PERSEVERANCE: Getting It Done
Helping children finish a job

• *Developmental Theme: Promote Good Daily Habits*

Parents can help their children learn to finish a job, an important skill for success in school and in life. For example, when you ask a child to do a job at home, make sure that the job is completed.

Suppose you ask your child to clear the table after dinner. You notice that several items remain on the table.

Without getting angry, say, "You aren't quite finished with your job. There are things on the table that need to be put away. When you are finished, you can play."

It might seem easier to do the job yourself. But when you don't ask children to finish, they don't learn how to complete a job.

21 PERSEVERANCE: Signaling for Help
Helping children learn to ask for help appropriately

• *Developmental Theme: Personal Competency*

Supporting your children while they are completing assignments is a vital parental role during the early school years. While children are working, parents can give prompts, encouragement, praise, and feedback.

Sometimes parents may be busy and cannot stop what they are doing when a child asks for help. Using a silent signaling device can increase your child's ability to wait for help. It encourages your child to make good use of time by moving on to the next problem or item.

Using an empty can, cover one half with red paper and the other half with green paper. If the red side is up, it is a signal that "I need help." If the green side is showing it means, "I am doing it on my own" or "I'm working."

In school, children have to learn to wait for their turn, the teacher's attention, and getting supplies. Learning to take turns is an important skill that helps build success in school and in life.

22 *CARING: Interview Magic*

• *Developmental Theme: Create and Imagine*

WHY DO IT

This activity gives your child undivided attention and provides an opportunity for him to think about good personal qualities.

MATERIALS

Paper
Pencil
Pretend or play microphone

HOW TO DO IT

Have your child pretend that he has become a famous person. Ask questions, listen carefully, and take notes as if you are an interviewing reporter.

Ask:

- What is your full name?
- Where do you live?
- How many people live in your house?
- What is your favorite animal?
- What makes you laugh?
- What do you want to do when you grow up?

ANOTHER IDEA

Reverse roles and have your child interview you or another member of the family. Let your child make up the questions to ask.

 Learn more about your family, present and past. Go on a "scavenger hunt" for family members. Do you know anyone in the family who speaks more than one language? Has anyone been in a play? Is anyone more than eighty years old?

23 CARING: Those Who Help

• *Developmental Theme: Connect with Others*

WHY DO IT
Good deeds that help others in the community make you and your child feel good.

MATERIALS
Newspaper or magazine articles

HOW TO DO IT
Together with your child read an article about a good deed someone has done. Talk about what that person did. Was it difficult? Tell your child about people you know who have helped their community.

Did you ever think of doing something helpful for someone, and then not do it? How did you feel about it? Do you think people help each other enough? Why or why not?

ANOTHER IDEA
Ask your child to think of at least two things that can be done to help someone. Help your child pick a good deed to do for someone. Do the action and talk about what happened and how it made your child feel.

 Talk with your child about people who have become famous for helping others, like Martin Luther King, Sojourner Truth, Florence Nightingale, and Mother Teresa. Go to the library and get a biography of someone who supported others. Read and discuss the book together.

24 *CARING: What's Important to You?*
Choosing people over things

• *Developmental Theme: Create and Imagine*

With your child, make a list of very important things that it would be hard to live without. The choices might include objects such as TV, computer, a bike, or a car. Include people such as family and friends. Make the list as long as you can.

After talking about what your child has listed, review the list again. Ask your child to cross out the items that are not that important. Let your child make judgments about what should be kept on the list.

Help your child to understand that family and friends are hard to replace and are very important—more important than things.

25 TEAMWORK: Follow, Lead, and Join

• *Developmental Theme: Listen, Speak, and Do*

WHY DO IT

Listening is an important part of learning. Children can be taught to listen not just for what they want to hear. This activity teaches your child how to listen and how to follow directions.

HOW TO DO IT

During any daily activity, ask your child to observe and tell you what you are both doing. Examples include crossing the street, talking to another person, turning right, and looking down.

Decide to do something without telling your child what it is. It may be going to the park, mailing a letter, or walking to the store. Have your child walk ahead of you, following the directions to the unknown destination you give until you arrive at the spot.

ANOTHER IDEA

Take turns and have your child give you directions to follow. Have your child choose several of the home activities that she has enjoyed doing with you. Talk about these.

There are many ways that listening and speaking are developed in daily life. Good listening skills develop positive habits for school success and also help you at home.

26 *TEAMWORK: Fun File Box*
Helping children keep track of free events

• *Developmental Theme: Reach Out and Explore*

Check for events and places to visit in your community, especially those that are free, and try to attend these regularly.

Decorate a small box with your child. Write on it, "Places We've Visited, Things We've Done." Get a local map. Mark the map with a star for each place you go or event you attend.

Attach a note, postcard, snapshot, or child's drawing to a file card that tells about the place or activity. Place it into the fun file box.

After you have several items in the box, examine them with your child and relive family fun times.

27 TEAMWORK: Whose Turn Is It?

• *Developmental Theme: Listen, Speak, and Do*

WHY DO IT

Household tasks get done better and faster when they are divided fairly among members of the family. Knowing how to divide tasks and organize them helps children do better in school, too.

MATERIALS

Pencil or pen
Paper

HOW TO DO IT

Together, pick some household tasks that have several parts. A good example is preparing a meal. Make a list of the steps. What do you do first? What comes next? Your list of steps might look like this:

- Planning the meal
- Shopping for the food
- Cooking the food
- Setting the table
- Serving the meal
- Cleaning up afterwards

Ask each family member to choose and do one job on the list. Share tasks with younger children to get them involved. This develops a strong team effort.

ANOTHER IDEA

Have your family think of other jobs that can be done together, both at home and outside of the home. Children can move on to more teamwork tasks after they learn to do the easier ones.

Think of a project your family can do together to help the community, the church, or the school. Plan it and do it together. These projects can include collecting food for the needy, recycling papers and bottles, or serving in a soup kitchen.

28 COMMON SENSE: Know, Choose, and Succeed

• *Developmental Theme: Personal Competency*

WHY DO IT
It's important to develop a plan for an emergency.

MATERIALS
Paper
Marker

HOW TO DO IT
Write the word EMERGENCY at the top of a piece of paper. Just below this word write Fire, Police, and Ambulance in three columns. Put a picture of a fire below the word Fire. Put pictures of a police car and ambulance below Police and Ambulance.

   With your child, look up the emergency numbers for Fire and Police. These are listed in the front of the telephone book. Fill in the emergency number under the column headings.

ANOTHER IDEA
Add more numbers for the doctor's office, Dad's work, Mom's work, and any friends or relatives to be called in an emergency.

 Practice what your child should do if there is an emergency. With your finger on the end call button, help your child dial the correct phone numbers and speak clearly to the operator. Have your child give the home address, phone number, and request the help that is needed. Practice until your child feels secure in being able to act quickly in an emergency.

29 COMMON SENSE: Charting a Course

• *Developmental Theme: Pre-Read and Respond*

WHY DO IT

This activity helps your child develop an understanding of sequence and the directions north, south, east, and west.

MATERIALS

Paper
Marker
Map

HOW TO DO IT

With your child, make up a story about a trip. Decide on a topic and take turns, adding one sentence at a time. The first sentence might begin, "Once upon a time a boy lived in a land way up north."

Mark north, south, east, and west on a map. Help your child create directions to go to one of the places on the map.

Locate where relatives or friends live and mark the locations. Plan a trip to visit one of the places and have your child give directions.

ANOTHER IDEA

Use a road map to plan a family trip. Have your child find the best route. Practice phrases such as "Here is where we start. Here is where we will finish our trip. Which direction do we travel? North? South? East? West?"

Post ideas for activities or trips so that family members have time to think about them.

30 COMMON SENSE: Operation Alert

• *Developmental Theme: Promote Good Daily Habits*

WHY DO IT

This activity helps children recognize warning labels on medicines and household cleaners.

MATERIALS

Paper
Pen or pencil
Old newspapers
Sturdy box
Four or five household products and medicines

HOW TO DO IT

Spread newspapers on a flat surface. Take household products from a box, one at a time. Ask your child to find the warning labels and try to read them with your help. Make a list of the words that mean WATCH OUT. Some of these are caution, poison, danger, warning, and hazard. Point out the skull and crossbones symbols.

Discuss why these household products and medicines are kept out of everyone's reach. Return the products to a safe place and talk about why they should never be opened and used without adult help.

ANOTHER IDEA

Talk about what can be done if household products are swallowed accidentally. The labels tell us what remedies to take to work against the poison. These are called "antidotes."

 Put your child's list of warning words in a special place for the family to see.

31 COMMON SENSE: Our TV Plan

• *Developmental Theme: Promote Good Daily Habits*

WHY DO IT
This activity gets the whole family involved in making choices about TV watching.

MATERIALS
TV schedule
Marker

HOW TO DO IT
As a family, decide how many hours a day that you will watch TV. Read the TV schedule aloud with your child and share your opinions about the shows that you like. Children need to hear your judgments. Pick shows to watch and circle them.

Go on a TV diet as a family. If you are watching TV four hours a day now, cut back to three hours a day the first week. Decrease the number of hours the second week and so on. Fill the extra time with outdoor activities, family fun and game time, doing exercises, and completing chores together.

ANOTHER IDEA
Decide with your child on a reward for keeping the TV time limit for at least three days. The reward could be materials for a hobby or other favorite activity, a special time with you, making a craft together, watching a movie together, etc. The best reward is that family members will have more time to play, learn, and be together.

 If this plan doesn't work all the way, it at least does part of the job. It raises the awareness of how much time your family is spending in front of the TV. That can be enough to change some TV watching and computer habits.

32 PROBLEM SOLVING: Give Us the Facts

• *Developmental Theme: Think and Organize*

WHY DO IT
Solving math problems leads to solving problems in everyday life and sharpens your child's thinking and reasoning skills.

MATERIALS
Paper
Pen or pencil

HOW TO DO IT
Think of how numbers are used in everyday situations such as the telephone, transportation schedules, and clothing sizes. Try to think of as many situations as you can.

Talk about what would happen if there were no numbers. How would we tell time? What would an address look like? What would we use for money? List the ways numbers help us.

ANOTHER IDEA
Traveling is part of everyday life. We can use numbers to determine the distance we travel. Check the car's odometer before you start and after a short trip. Write the two numbers and show your child how to use subtraction to find how far you traveled.

 Talk about the importance of thinking and reasoning skills. How are these abilities helpful in job and family situations? When your child uses good thinking and reasoning skills, praise what you hear and see.

33 PROBLEM SOLVING: What Job Is That?

• *Developmental Theme: Connect with Others*

WHY DO IT

Good habits created when children are young can help them do well in the workplace later. This activity teaches your child about work in the world.

MATERIALS

Newspaper classified ads section
Pen or pencil
Paper

HOW TO DO IT

Help your child find and cut out three advertisements for jobs. With your child, read the ads aloud.

Compare the ads to find:

- What are the qualifications needed?
- How do you apply for the job?
- Which one pays the highest salary?

Talk about how habits that are developed now will help get and keep a job later. Examples are being on time, dressing neatly, and listening carefully. Turning in sloppy work, not being helpful, and being rude are negative behavior patterns.

ANOTHER IDEA

Ask your child, "Have you started thinking about jobs you would like to have when you are grown up? Do we know someone who has this job? Will you work hard enough and read enough to give you the skills for the job you want?"

 Assure your child that it is always a good time to build good habits. Help your child recognize that a willingness to face and solve problems is an important step in change.

34 PROBLEM SOLVING: What Would You Do?

• *Developmental Theme: Personal Competency*

WHY DO IT

This activity helps your child practice solving everyday problems at home and at school.

HOW TO DO IT

Talk with your child about problems that you are facing that are small or big. These might include having two appointments at the same time, the car needing repairs, or having a family member who is ill. You can help your child learn ways to deal with everyday problems by brainstorming. This means naming as many ways as possible to solve a problem.

Pretend the following happened. Ask your child what to do if:

- He gets lost while shopping with his parents.
- He is playing outside. A car stops and someone in the car tells him to "come on over."

Make up other situations that are real problems. Ask your child to brainstorm solutions.

ANOTHER IDEA

Trade places. Ask your child for a problem for you to solve. Talk about the pros and cons of the solutions you share.

 When children practice solving problems before they are faced with them, they develop stronger thinking skills.

35 *PROBLEM SOLVING: Scoring and Mapping*

Learning to read a newspaper and use a map

• *Developmental Theme: Listen, Speak, and Do*

This activity provides practice in reading, math, and geography.

Read the sports page of the newspaper with your child. Let your child sound out the team names and talk about who won and by how much. Calculate the difference in the scores. Talk about which teams won by the most points.

Locate the team cities on a map. Mark the map to show the locations. Ask your child to tell you if the teams are near or far away.

Choose a favorite team. Make banners for your favorite teams and check their scores regularly to see how they are doing.

36 *FOCUS: Your Child's Own Map*

• *Developmental Theme: Create and Imagine*

WHY DO IT

This activity helps children gain practical knowledge for everyday living.

MATERIALS

Large sheet of paper
Colored markers

HOW TO DO IT

Place a large sheet of paper on the floor. Ask your child to draw a picture of your home in the center of the paper and title the map with a name. Draw your street. Write the street name and your house and telephone numbers.

Have your child place an X on the map to mark important places in the neighborhood.

- Your child's school
- A nearby store
- The home of a helpful neighbor or nearest relative
- The fire, police, or rescue station

Talk with your child about which place is nearest your home and which is farthest. Make guesses. Don't worry about exact distances between places. Encourage your child to put other places on this personal map. Post the map on the refrigerator, on the washing machine, or on the window for everyone to look at and use.

ANOTHER IDEA

Get or make a local map of your area and help your child locate your neighborhood. Mark this map with the places your child has chosen for the personal map. Discuss map scale and why the distances to places look different.

 Helping your child focus on results, not perfection, is an important skill for higher achievement.

37 *FOCUS: Memory Matters*
Helping children remember and use information

• Developmental Theme: Reach Out and Explore

Knowing how to recall and use information from past events is an important part of common sense. Ask your child questions such as these:

- What did you eat for Lunch? Breakfast? Dinner last night?
- Go back to yesterday and see what you can remember.
- Who did you play with?
- What did you read at school?

Ask your child to make up questions for you to try to answer. You may find that your child is better at this game than you are.

38 *FOCUS: Should I? Maybe Not!*
Helping children make decisions

• Developmental Theme: Think and Organize

Almost everything we do is the result of decisions we make, such as being on time, helping others, and showing consideration.

Ask your child to think of a time when there was a problem to solve and the response was, "I couldn't help it," "Something made me do it," or "It's not my fault." There are times when things cannot be helped or changed, but they are not as frequent as we might think.

Ask your child what would have been a better way to tackle the problem. Discuss the importance of looking at the positives and the negatives of a solution before making a decision. Using this method makes a choice easier.

Hasty decisions made before examining both sides of a problem can lead to bad experiences. A second, more critical, look into an unpleasant situation helps us see what we might have done.

39 RESPECT: Hug Yourself

• *Developmental Theme: Connect with Others*

WHY DO IT

This activity encourages children to think about what makes them special.

HOW TO DO IT

Help your child to complete these sentences:

- If I were a car, I would be _____.
- If I were a TV character, I would be _____.
- If I were an athlete, I would be _____.
- If I were a place, I would be _____.

Ask your child to think about other ideas to add. Take turns answering the sentences.

ANOTHER IDEA

Help your child to make comparisons. Try the following:

- Am I more like a pizza or a salad?
- Am I more like a bicycle or a car?
- Am I more like a basketball or a beach ball?
- Am I more like a butterfly or a bumblebee?

Add your own ideas and take turns making choices. Explain to each other why you made your choices.

Children learn in different ways and at different rates. They learn from the examples of adults in their lives. Helping a child identify, develop, and use their distinctive abilities promotes success in school and in life.

40 RESPECT: Say It in Writing

• Developmental Theme: Pre-Read and Respond

WHY DO IT

Communicating with your child verbally and in writing helps build feelings of respect and lets your child know that you care.

MATERIALS

Paper
Marker
Pencil

HOW TO DO IT

Write a riddle or joke on a napkin and put it inside your child's lunch box. Your child can share it with friends at school.

At bedtime your child can leave a private voice mail message for you at work. You get clues about what's on her mind and in her heart. If possible, leave messages for your child on a home voice mail.

ANOTHER IDEA

While your child gets ready for bed, place a special "good night" message on her pillow. Encourage her to do the same for you.

 As an incentive for your child to keep the messages coming, share a "mystery" note every few days, praising your child and letting her guess who sent it.

41 *RESPECT: What Makes People Tick?*

• *Developmental Theme: Connect with Others*

WHY DO IT
This activity increases children's awareness and understanding of the similarities and differences among people.

MATERIALS
Pen or Pencil
Paper
Map

HOW TO DO IT
Talk about each family member and how they are similar and different. Think about someone you saw recently who is different from yourself, such as a homeless person carrying bundles or a person in a wheelchair. With your child, try to imagine what it feels like to be that person.

Talk about the problems people face and how they cope with them. Talk with your child about ways to understand and be helpful to others who have special needs.

ANOTHER IDEA
Think about ways to learn more about people from different countries. Do this by talking to neighbors who might be from a foreign country, taking books out of the library, checking TV programs, and reading newspapers. As you find facts about other countries, use a map to mark the country.

 We are interconnected in many ways with other countries and cultures. Children encounter many different people and languages in school. Developing an appreciation of others and their strengths will help your child be more successful in this global age.

42 RESPECT: Watch Your Language
Being thoughtful of others with language

• *Developmental Theme: Listen, Speak, and Do*

Off-color language can easily become part of your child's vocabulary if you are not careful. Your child watches and copies your behavior. If you blurt out an obscenity, apologize for the slipup and tell your child what you meant to say using appropriate language.

Consider a penalty if your child catches you swearing. It might be a quarter in the piggy bank. Do not give up. It can take a long time before a bad habit is broken.

Your child's mind is like a camera phone that records what is seen and heard. Make sure that your home is the most positive environment your child can experience.

10

Look, Listen, and Do MegaSkills

• For Children Who Need More Practice

"The reward for work well done is the opportunity to do more."

—Jonas Salk
developer of the polio vaccine

MEGASKILL	ACTIVITY NAME
Confidence	Being a Star, Dressing By "The Words"
Motivation	Taking Care of Me
Effort	Noting Numbers
Responsibility	Healthy Habits
Initiative	My Place
Perseverance	I Want To Do It
Caring	Now and Then
Teamwork	Exercise and Numbers
Common Sense	Solving Problems In Advance
Problem Solving	Stocking the Store
Focus	Family Days, Go With the Maps
Respect	Having an A+ Attitude

Look, Listen, and Do MegaSkills: For Children Who Need Extra Practice

This chapter includes tested activities that turn everyday experiences into enriching, individualized exercises to promote growth in reading, writing, and math. These activities are unique in that they integrate perceptual skills with life skills that children need for success. Each activity strengthens children's visual skills (look), auditory skills (listen), and body movement skills (do).

Building language abilities is the key theme for each activity. They are designed to elicit active responses from children of a wide age range, from preschool to early elementary.

Tips on Using Look, Listen, and Do MegaSkills

Pick activities in any order you wish. Read through the entire activity first. Depending on your child's learning needs, you may decide to do only one part of an activity to provide practice in a particular area, such as visual or auditory learning.

You may need to repeat the words you are asking your child to respond to. Do so freely and take your time. Give lots of examples and provide frequent positive feedback. Use questions to focus your child's attention. To gain the most benefit from these activities, do them often.

1 *Being a Star*

Building a child's confidence by putting on a show.

● *MegaSkill: CONFIDENCE*

Get Ready!

You will need a magazine or newspaper that can be rolled into a make-believe megaphone. Clear floor space to use as a stage. Have handy some poster paper and markers or crayons.

Plan the special announcement that you will use to present your child. "Ladies and gentlemen I would like to present to you _____" or "Today, we are pleased to have with us _____ performing_____."

Eyes

Ask your child to look directly at the audience. It might be just you or a neighbor or two. Your child can choose something to share, such as a poem, a riddle, a song, a picture book, some words just learned, a tumbling stunt, etc. Your child practices the choice "offstage" until a level of comfort is reached. Then introduce your child to the audience. The show is on! Clapping and praise follow.

Ears

As your child gains confidence, the spoken part of the performance can be lengthened. Ask your child to explain how to do something. This might include how to use a toy, how to play dress-up, how to learn a new game, etc.

Hands

Ask your child to make a poster with drawings about the performance: date, time, name of shows. Hang this poster for all to see.

2 *Dressing by "The Words"*
Learning and using words that describe clothing

• *MegaSkill: CONFIDENCE*

Get Ready!

Gather some clothes together, perhaps a pile ready for washing.

Eyes

Children can dress themselves with a few good words from you. Introduce the words "shirt," "sock," "shoe," "pants," "shorts," etc. to your child. Place your child's clothing for the day on the bed.

Make getting dressed into a game. Ask, "Can you find your shirt?" Your child can look for the shirt and put it on, with your delight and help as needed.

Ears

Talk about the color of clothes and the idea of matching. Ask your child to name and describe each piece of clothing and tell where it goes on the body.

After your child puts on the item of clothing, say aloud the body part it covers, such as foot, arm, head, over the knee, on the shoulder, etc. Repeat the parts as needed. Have your child repeat the names of the body parts and point to them.

Hands

With your child, label closets and drawers so that items of clothing are easy to find.

Ask your child to draw pictures of the clothes on the labels. Try masking tape for these labels on the drawers. Masking tape usually leaves no marks.

Encourage your child to choose clothing for the next day. Discuss which choices may be more appropriate than others. Check to see that all needed items are selected.

3 Taking Care of Me
Practicing self-reliance

• MegaSkill: MOTIVATION

Get Ready!

Get the soap ready. Children need to be able to take care of their own personal grooming and know the feeling of being clean.

Eyes

Next to the bathroom sink, post a check-off chart with the days of the week. Attach pencil or crayon with a string. Include tasks such as:

- I brushed my teeth.
- I washed my face.
- I combed my hair.

Ask your child to do each of the tasks noted on the chart and check off the boxes when they are complete.

Ears

Check the chart and say aloud all of the activities listed. Ask your child to listen carefully and repeat them after you. Trade places. Your child says the activities, and you repeat them. Ask your child to listen hard and ask, "Did I do it right?"

Hands

Have your child make the next chart. Add a bedroom to the chart with new boxes to check, such as:

- I picked up my clothes.
- I put my clothes into the laundry basket.
- I made my bed.
- I put away my toys.

This activity encourages your child to monitor self-behavior, and it also helps with personal grooming and chores. Your child starts with small steps and moves toward more complex activities.

4 Noting Numbers
Learning to recognize and retrieve numbers

• *MegaSkill: EFFORT*

Get Ready!
Assemble newspapers and other objects that have numbers on them.

Eyes
Walk through the house with your child and point to objects with numbers, such as the clock, pages of a book, and the calendar.

Ask your child to pick one object with numbers and try to picture it with his eyes closed. Then have him look at the object again, find two numbers to remember, say them aloud, and then say them in reverse order.

Look at the inside and outside of things to find numbers. Examples: clothing tags, inside shoes, on the TV remote. Discuss what the numbers mean.

Ears
When children use numbers in everyday situations, it leads to interest in basic computation skills. With your child, name some of the ways numbers are used in daily life. Examples: the weather report, sports news, paying bills, telling time, shopping for groceries. Say some of these numbers aloud. Ask your child to repeat these in the order you said them.

Hands
Cut large numbers from cardboard. Pick numbers that hold meaning: family ages, your house address, telephone numbers. Large printed numbers actually make lovely decorations. Move them about in new combinations and put them back together again.

5 *Healthy Habits*
Building the base for good health and safety practices

• *MegaSkill: RESPONSIBILITY*

Get Ready!

Talk about good health, safety, and exercise habits. Examples: washing hands, brushing teeth, jogging. Collect several magazines with pictures of these activities.

Eyes

Together, look through magazines and find pictures of people doing activities to keep healthy. These include walking outside, eating nutritious foods, and exercising.

With your child find (or draw) pictures of people doing activities to be safer. Examples: taking toys off the stairs and crossing the street at the corner.

Ears

Think of this as an easy exercise plan for you and your child to follow for a few days. Each day you will do more:

Day One. Bounce a ball five times. Jump in place ten times. Jog for one minute.

Day Two: Bounce the ball ten times. Jump in place ten times. Jog for two minutes.

You and your child can time one another. Count together to be sure that each of you is doing your part.

Hands

Help your child list three health/safety reminders. Use as few words as possible. Use big letters. Examples: brush teeth, pick up toys.

With your child, place health and safety reminders near the places where good habits need to be practiced such as a "WASH HANDS" sign at the sink.

6 *My Place*

Teaching children ways to organize materials.

• *MegaSkill: INITIATIVE*

Get Ready!

Together, make a list of items used in arts and crafts, such as pencils, markers, and paper. Gather together a variety of these items.

Eyes

Place all the items in one pile. Ask your child to separate the pencils and the crayons. Ask your child to pick a long pencil and a short one. Ask your child to group all the long pencils together; group all of the short ones together.

Choose one crayon and ask your child to find the crayons that are of the same or similar color.

Ears

List the steps needed to make a personal school or crafts box. Say the steps in order:

Ask your child to listen carefully and repeat the steps in the same order. Give one direction at a time. For example, "Bring your box of crayons." Then trade places. Let your child give you a direction to follow.

Hands

Find a box to hold art supplies. Place your child's name on the top of the box and encourage her to decorate it. Use a ruler to measure the box. Cut pieces of wrapping paper to fit each side. Paste or tape the paper to the sides of the box.

Fill the box with art supplies, such as scraps of material, colored paper, etc. Put the box in a special "reminding" place. It will help your child to find what she needs on her own for crafts at home.

7 *I Want to Do It*
Taking time to do a specific project

• *MegaSkill: PERSEVERANCE*

Get Ready!

You will need magazines with pictures, scissors, paste, a marker, and a large piece of paper.

Eyes

Have your child look through magazines and cut out pictures of people doing indoor and outdoor activities. Then ask your child to name which ones are done indoors and which ones are done outdoors. For example, vacuuming is done indoors. Running is done outdoors.

Look through magazines together to select pictures that show activities your family enjoys, such as singing, swimming, camping, etc. Encourage your child to make a poster of these "likes." Write a title on the paper and post it for the family to enjoy.

Ears

With your child, name and talk about the activities shown in the pictures. Ask your child to pick one. Make a plan and a time to do this activity together.

Hands

Mix up the pictures and ask your child to put the pictures in separate piles. For example, outdoor activities in one pile, indoor activities in another. You and your child can think of other ways the pictures can be separated. This is called "classification."

8 *Now and Then*
Learning about family history to develop good feelings and pride

• *MegaSkill: CARING*

Get Ready!
Gather some family photographs, a roll of shelf paper, paste, and markers.

Eyes
With your child, spread out the family snapshots on a roll of paper. Start with early days to the present. Talk together about what your child sees in the pictures. Make a mark about every twelve inches on the shelf paper. Put a number on it. Together, point to the markers for the photos to be pasted at the youngest years. Along with your child, put the pictures in order to match the numbers.

Ears
Talk to your child about each photo. Ask your child to listen and tell:

- Who is in the picture?
- What color clothes are worn?
- Was the picture taken inside the house or outdoors?
- Where and when was the picture taken?

Ask your child: Can you guess how old you were when this photograph was taken?

Hands
Your child draws lines between the pictures pasted on the roll of paper. Cut along the lines so that each picture is separated. Mix up the pictures. Ask your child to place them in order from youngest days to now. This activity is a real memory builder.

9 *Exercise and Numbers*

Developing a child's ability to follow directions combined with numbers

• *MegaSkill: TEAMWORK*

Get Ready!

Find some comfortable clothes for this activity. Choose a place indoors that is safe for jumping and turn on some music. When the weather is good, go outdoors.

Eyes

Show several play objects to your child, such as a ball, a jump rope, and a sand bucket. Say the name of each object aloud. Choose an object and do an exercise with it. Ask your child to watch and imitate your exercise. Then your child can choose an object and do an exercise for you to imitate.

Ears

Bounce a ball on three different surfaces, such as rug, wood, metal, and tile. Say the surface name aloud. Then ask your child to close his eyes as you bounce the ball again. Can he name the surface now?

Bounce the ball in a rhythmic pattern. For example, two bounces on one surface and one on another. Ask your child to listen carefully and tell when the sounds are the same or different. Then trade places. Now you listen hard as your child bounces the ball.

Hands

Place the objects (ball, rope, bucket, etc.) around the room. Give directions for your child to find and bring an object from another part of the room. Do not use the object's name. For example, say "Go to the back of the room and find something that is round and red." Then direct your child to bring the object back hopping or skipping. Try trading places as well. It multiplies the fun!

10 *Solving Problems in Advance*
Playing "what would I do?" games

• *MegaSkill: COMMON SENSE*

Get Ready!

Think up an assortment of questions you can ask your child about situations related to school, home, holidays, or emergencies. Ask your child, "What would you do if...?"

Eyes

...You see a friend playing with one of your favorite toys?
...You are in the mall and you find someone's wallet?

Ears

...You are home alone and hear a knock at the door?
...You are asleep and the smoke detector goes off?
...You hit a ball that dents a neighbor's car?

Hands

...You are watching television and your mother asks you to help set the table?
...You are riding your bike, fall off, and are hurt and bleeding?

> Note: Encourage more discussion by asking, "What else might you do?" "Can you think of other ideas to solve the problem?" "Why would you choose to do that?" "What if that didn't work?" You can give your best solution and ask your child to tell you if that is a good one.

11 Stocking the Store
Using language to buy items in a play or real store

• *MegaSkill: PROBLEM SOLVING*

Get Ready!

Save empty milk cartons, cans, and boxes to create your child's own home store. You and your child can pretend to buy or sell these items.

Eyes

Go together to the supermarket and ask your child to find an item (on a low shelf) that you describe. Note: When cartons are empty, they can be used for a play store at home.

Ears

Say the names of two grocery products aloud and ask your child to repeat them. Trade places. Have your child name the products and you repeat their names. Keep adding items to build stronger listening and memory skills.

Hands

Look carefully at your grocery cupboards at home. With your child, draw a plan for ways to use the space. Fill in where you will put cans, boxes, etc.

Label the cupboard shelf by type of items. For example, vegetables, cereals, pet food, etc. Children will be able to use this plan to help you put away groceries.

12 *Family Days*
Learning how to use a calendar

• *MegaSkill: FOCUS*

Get Ready!

Buy or draw a month-by-month calendar. A marker and sticky notes will be handy, too.

Eyes

Point out two different months on the calendar. Ask your child to compare the months: How many days are in each month? What letter does each month start with?

Point to the date of the first Tuesday in each month. Is the date for the first Tuesday the same in both months? What else is different in the two months?

Ears

Look at the calendar with your child and name the months of summer: June, July, and August. Then ask your child to name two months starting with the letter J.

Name three activities and family birthdays for at least one month and ask your child to repeat them. Name the dates for Thanksgiving, Christmas, and New Year's Eve and ask your child to repeat the dates and find them on the calendar.

Hands

Make or buy a calendar. Record family birthdays, appointments, special events, and vacations. Ask your child to participate and remind you to help keep the calendar up-to-date.

13 *Go with the Maps*
Learning about directions and map reading

• *MegaSkill: FOCUS*

Get Ready!

Get a map of your community from a library, car rental company, or local chamber of commerce, or print one off the Internet.

Eyes

Spread the map out on a flat surface. Orient the map so that from your child's point of view, north (N) is at the top and south (S) is at the bottom.

Ask your child to point out different colors on the map, one at a time. Find the colors that are the same. Find the symbol for railroad tracks. Do the same for other symbols, such as rivers, highways, etc.

Ask your child to find a place to visit. Try to arrange a trip to this place.

Ears

Name two streets near your home. Repeat these names several times.

Say: "I'm going to say the names of one park, one river, and one street. Listen and tell me when you hear the street name."

Point to the directions. Then cover the map and ask: Where is north? south? east? west? Let your child test you, too.

Hands

Together find on the map the streets where your family and your child's friends live. Ask your child to locate and point to nearby attractions. Start the game by saying: "We live on _____ Street." Point out parks and rivers etc. Say these aloud. Then say, "Your friend _____ lives on _____ Street." Ask your child to point to and name these.

14 Having an A+ Attitude
Spreading positive attitudes throughout the family

• *MegaSkill: RESPECT*

Get Ready!

Think about this: When polite feelings are expressed from one family member to another, your child is more likely to copy these expressions and use polite words and actions.

Eyes

Taking care of a pet can be part of a child's responsibility. Talk about the necessary steps, such as giving food and water, cleaning up, etc.

Draw pictures or write the steps to help your child remember. You can avoid a lot of unpleasant words later, such as "I didn't know I was supposed to do that."

Ears

When children are thanked for meeting their responsibilities, they are more likely to thank others. Share the thanks aloud. It shows that you notice and appreciate your child's contributions. Gratitude and praise are contagious. Your child will recall your kind words long after you have said them.

Hands

When your child is given a job such as counter-wiping, help her develop self-respect. Show her how the job should be done. Then, step back and let her do it. Accept her best effort. If touch-ups are really needed, do them when she is not present.

Reminder: We are all scientists, with or without degrees. We try to learn a little bit more each day and use this new learning in new ways. It's the wonder and the challenge of education...and all the practice it takes!

- Getting the Best from Technology

11

Tech Tips

"My childhood should have taught me lessons for my own fatherhood, but it didn't because parenting can only be learned by people who have no children."
—Bill Cosby, comedian

1 CONFIDENCE
Feeling able to do it

When you select computer games and software for your child, look for those that offer thoughtful, idea-generating activities. Try to avoid the one-dimensional "click and find the bird" games.

The software you choose should help your child develop and use the computer on a number of levels. Just as with a good toy, you want computer materials that extend your child's abilities and that give you both lots to talk about.

Check the internet for education sites offering advice on choosing software for children.

2 MOTIVATION
Wanting to do it

Try not to "surf" the Internet aimlessly. It can be a big waste of time. Encourage even young children to have a goal when they are using the computer.

To add direction and motivation to working with the Internet, help your child to identify one new area or subject to learn about each week.

Follow your own good advice. With your child, pick subjects for mom or dad to learn about and check out websites together.

You can pick almost any topic to learn more about—from prehistoric dinosaurs to current favorite books. You may want to follow the weather daily or find out about sports heroes. It will be fascinating to jump from website to website to find out as much as you can.

3 EFFORT
Being willing to work hard

Clicking on the mouse and moving from website to website is easy. But it takes a lot of computer engineering to make this possible.

If you are familiar with the technology, share with your child what you know about how computers work and how software is created. If computers are a big mystery to you (like they are to many of us), then look up some basic information about how they work and share this with your child.

Help your child connect the information about the computer to real-life, everyday computer uses. Talk about computers at the bank, on airplanes, and even in cars.

4 RESPONSIBILITY
Doing what's right

The computer can be the cause of a lot of irresponsible behavior, with material on many websites that young children should avoid. Parents need to monitor their child's computer use, sitting nearby.

Some websites can simply be declared off-limits, just like certain TV programs. Others can be removed from the range of child choices. Find out how to protect your child's safety on the Web by visiting www.protectkids.com and its sister site www.enough.org. The FBI also has an informational guide for parents at www. fbi.org.

Better yet, start early to help your child develop his own judgment about wholesome websites to visit. Talk about why certain websites are more responsible than others.

5 INITIATIVE
Moving into action

Spark initiative by setting up a family website. For help building a family website, visit www.myfamily.org, www.familylobby.com, or www.familyland.com. Your first site is an experiment. You can keep adding and subtracting from your site as your family and your experience grows.

Work with your child to post pictures and captions. Keep it up-to-date and link it with other family members' pages. Ask your child to dictate to you what he wants to say on the page. Read these words aloud with your child.

This is the modern version of a family newsletter and can be the holiday letter that gets sent all year long. Strangers may not be interested, but parents and grandparents can be counted on to read it.

6 PERSEVERANCE
Completing what you start

Computers are great teachers of perseverance. They offer untold frustration that we have to overcome. One wrong move and the computer goes down, and we struggle and persevere to bring it back into operation. Just waiting to get on the Web or to print a page or two can be a lesson in perseverance.

Give your child a chance to experience these frustrations with you. Don't spare them. Let your child give you the support and solace you need as you struggle to get back online.

7 CARING
Showing concern for others

Work with your child to find safe websites and discussion groups. Find sites with information about subjects and stories about people, not just games or ads.

Start email correspondence with friends and family. Your child can dictate letters that show caring for relatives and friends. Receiving an email message is almost as good as getting a "real" letter.

8 TEAMWORK
Working with others

Sit with your child in front of the computer as you explore the Internet. Talk about what you see. Share your opinions, observations, and judgments about the websites.

Urge your child to turn from the keyboard to talk with you about what he learns, and about questions he has. This is the real meaning of "interactive."

9 COMMON SENSE
Using good judgment

You may need to set up a computer schedule for your home. Spending too much time at the computer robs children of time for friends, play, and hobbies.

Be sure to remind your child that ads are still ads, whether they appear on the Internet, on TV, or in magazines. Children need to be just as wary of advertising on the Internet as in any other medium.

10 PROBLEM SOLVING
Putting what you know and what you can do into action

Children need to know that computers are not magic: They are not problem solvers. They don't replace our brains. Computers provide information to assist in our own problem solving process.

Show young children how you use the computer to find directions to a certain address. Show how you use Google or other search engines to find answers to specific questions, such as nearby bus routes and distances to far away planets.

Encourage your child to type a question into different search engines. What answers do you both learn?

11 *FOCUS*
Concentrating with a goal in mind

There is so much to be found on the Web. It can seem like a very strange land. When we know what we're looking for, it is a wondrous land. When we don't, we may become discouraged.

Start a list of favorite websites. You and your child can create your own map. This will help you stay on track, focused, and able to find what you both need.

12 *RESPECT*
Showing good behavior, courtesy, and appreciation

When there is one computer in the home, it can seem that everyone wants to use it at once. Children need to learn to respect others' rights, and how to share time. When children ask for help, they need to learn to wait and not expect help on demand.

Teach your child to be respectful when using the computer, to be careful with it and with the feelings of family members and friends.

12

MegaSkills
Measures

• Introducing MegaSkills Measures

In this section you will find three ways to see how you and your children are progressing along the road to MegaSkills.

About My Child

This measure helps you assess your child's MegaSkills and determine which ones are stronger and which ones need more support to develop.

About Parents—About Ourselves

This measure helps parents assess their child-rearing, child-educating MegaSkills. The idea is to identify all that we are doing right as well as the areas we want to support and strengthen.

From Last Week to Last Month to the Last School Year, these parent/caregiver checklists provide MegaSkills-building words and actions.

> Note: You may want to duplicate the MegaSkills Measures so that you can use them more than once.

MegaSkills Measure: Thinking About My Child

When parents and teachers across the nation are asked about the best they want for their children, their answers center on the cornerstones of character and achievement. They center on MegaSkills. Here are some ways to see how your child is progressing on the road to MegaSkills.

Confidence — Feeling Able to Do It!

MegaSkills Kids Checkpoints	Not Yet Enough	Sometimes	A Lot
When my child wants someone to play with, does she ask, even when she feels shy?			
When someone says, "You won't be able to do that," does my child say: "Let me try"?			
Does my child try to do things for himself and not always depend on others to do them?			

Here's Another Way My Child Shows Confidence: _____

_____

_____

_____

_____

Confidence Goal: I promise to help "grow" My Child's Confidence by:

_____

_____

_____

_____

_____

Motivation – Wanting To Do It!

MegaSkills Kids Checkpoints	Not Yet Enough	Sometimes	A Lot
When my child learns about something new, he says, "Tell me more about that."			
Most of the time, does my child reply with "Yes" more than "No"?			
Does my child keep trying to improve and do her best?			

Here's Another Way My Child Shows Motivation: _____

_____

_____

_____

_____

Motivation Goal: I promise to help "grow" My Child's Motivation by:

_____

_____

_____

_____

_____

Effort – Being Willing To Work Hard

MegaSkills Kids Checkpoints	Not Yet Enough	Sometimes	A Lot
When asked to make an effort, does my child say, "Sure, I'll do it"?			
When my child makes an effort and it doesn't work out, does she say, "I'll try again next time"?			

Here's Another Way My Child Shows Effort: _____

_____

_____

_____

_____

Confidence Goal: I promise to help "grow" My Child's Effort by:

_____

_____

_____

_____

_____

Responsibility – Doing What's Right

MegaSkills Kids Checkpoints	Not Yet Enough	Sometimes	A Lot
Does my child say, "Let me help"?			
Does my child try not to fight and be angry a lot?			
Does my child keep his room and his things in good shape...even when he'd rather be doing something else?			

Here's Another Way My Child Shows Responsibility: _____

_____

_____

_____

_____

Responsibility Goal: I promise to help "grow" My Child's Responsibility by:

_____

_____

_____

_____

_____

Initiative – Moving Into Action

MegaSkills Kids Checkpoints	Not Yet Enough	Sometimes	A Lot
Does my child say, "I have a good idea!" and then try to make the idea come true?			
Does my child get things done on time?			
Does my child try to get over disappointment?			
Does my child keep going after a setback?			

Here's Another Way My Child Shows Initiative: _____

_____

_____

_____

_____

Initiative Goal: I promise to help "grow" My Child's Initiative by:

_____

_____

_____

_____

_____

Perseverance – Completing What You Start

MegaSkills Kids Checkpoints	Not Yet Enough	Sometimes	A Lot
Does my child have patience to take the time to do something well?			
Does my child expect to be good at everything right away?			
Does my child finish what she starts...most of the time?			

Here's Another Way My Child Shows Perseverance: _____

_____

_____

_____

_____

Perseverance Goal: I promise to help "grow" My Child's Perseverance by:

_____

_____

_____

_____

_____

Caring – Showing Concern for Others

MegaSkills Kids Checkpoints	Not Yet Enough	Sometimes	A Lot
Does my child realize that what he says and does can make others feel sad or happy?			
Does my child say and do nice things to make others feel good?			
Does my child make fun of people who are different?			

Here's Another Way My Child Shows Caring: _____

_____

_____

_____

_____

Perseverance Goal: I promise to help "grow" My Child's Perseverance by:

_____

_____

_____

_____

_____

Teamwork — Working with Others

MegaSkills Kids Checkpoints	Not Yet Enough	Sometimes	A Lot
Do other kids want to play with my child?			
Does my child take the blame when she does something wrong...or does she try to blame others ?			
Does my child realize that he doesn't always have to get his own way?			

Here's Another Way My Child Shows Teamwork: _____

_____

_____

_____

_____

Teamwork Goal: I promise to help "grow" My Child's Teamwork by:

_____

_____

_____

_____

_____

Common Sense – Using Good Judgment

MegaSkills Kids Checkpoints	Not Yet Enough	Sometimes	A Lot
Can my child tell the difference between what's make-believe and what's real...in TV, computers, movies and books?			
Does my child think ahead...predicting what could happen if she does certain things?			
Does my child understand that his actions have results...and some can be dangerous?			

Here's Another Way My Child Shows Common Sense: _____

_____

_____

_____

_____

Common Sense Goal: I promise to help "grow" My Child's Common Sense by:

_____

_____

_____

_____

_____

Problem Solving – Putting What I Know And Can Do Into Action

MegaSkills Kids Checkpoints	Not Yet Enough	Sometimes	A Lot
Is my child able to ask for help... when help is needed to solve a problem?			
Does my child try not to feel sorry for herself when she has a problem?			
Is my child able to think of lots of ways to solve a problem and then try to choose the better way?			

Here's Another Way My Child Shows Problem Solving: _____

_____

_____

_____

_____

Problem Solving Goal: I promise to help "grow" My Child's Problem Solving by:

_____

_____

_____

_____

_____

Focus– Concentrating With a Goal In Mind

MegaSkills Kids Checkpoints	Not Yet Enough	Sometimes	A Lot
Does my child know how to pay attention without having to be told?			
Does my child try to keep his mind on what he is doing?			
Does my child figure out how to get her work done?			

Here's Another Way My Child Shows Focus: _____

_____

_____

_____

_____

Focus Goal: I promise to help "grow" My Child's Focus by:

_____

_____

_____

_____

_____

Respect – Showing Good Behavior, Courtesy, and Appreciation

MegaSkills Kids Checkpoints	Not Yet Enough	Sometimes	A Lot
Does my child resist talking or trying to make someone feel bad?			
Is my child respectful, considerate and courteous, even when not feeling like it.			
Do my children respect the rights of others just as they want other to respect their rights?			

Here's Another Way My Child Shows Respect: _____

_____

_____

_____

_____

Respect Goal: I promise to help "grow" My Child's Respect by:

_____

_____

_____

_____

_____

• *MegaSkills Measures: About Parents — About Ourselves*

We grade ourselves hard as parents. Of course, there is no way we can do everything right. In this MegaSkills Measure, the focus is on parent MegaSkills. These are the small, special moments between parent and child.

In the Measure, parents have the opportunity to identify and assess our own MegaSkills as expressed in the words and actions of everyday life—as best we can remember, over the last year, the last month, and the last week. These are MegaSkills Moments.

Keep in Mind

The point of these measures is to recognize and reward yourself for all that you are doing right. Every family has its own way of doing right. Keep adding to the Other line and filling in activities as you move through the year. The key is to keep figuring out more things you do right and to reward yourself for them.

Consider going over the results with your children, asking them what they think about your answers. Perhaps they will be harder on you, or perhaps they will think you've short changed yourself. It's bound to be a fascinating and useful conversation.

Note: You may want to duplicate the following pages before you use them so that you can use them more than once.

MegaSkills Moments: Last Week

Think back over the last week. Ask yourself, "To what extent did I do the following with my child?" It may be that you ate a meal together every day; it may be that you read together at night; it may be that you took walks together. You may have done one of these regularly and another not at all. It's not possible to do everything.

Last Week, I...	Once	More Than Once
Gave my child a hug.		
Took a walk with my child.		
Read to my child.		
Ate at least one meal a day with my child.		
Asked my child what happened during the day.		
Let my child hug me.		
Told my child about my day.		
Watched a TV program with my child.		
Told my child I love him/her.		
Talked with my child about his/her friends.		
Played a quiet game indoors with my child.		
Played active sports outdoors with my child.		
Checked/regulated the time my child watches TV.		
Praised and encouraged my child.		
Did some household chores with my child.		
Cooked with my child.		
Other:		

Notes to myself: _____

_____

_____

The book *MegaSkills* contains a longer, more detailed version of this measure.

MegaSkills Moments: Last Month

Think back over the last month. Ask yourself, "To what extent did I do the following with on behalf of my child?"

Last Month, I...	Once	More Than Once
Encouraged my child to have friends visit our house.		
Spent time with my child on a hobby or special project over a period of several days.		
Listened to my child explain his/her point of view that was different from mine.		
Told my child about my own childhood experiences.		
Took my child to a church, library, museum, or zoo.		
Attended a play, concert, movie, sports event, or other entertainment with my child.		
Attended a play, concert, movie, sports event, or other entertainment with my child.		
Did something my child persuaded me to do that turned out to be a good idea.		
Read with my child.		
Other.		

Notes to myself: _____

_____

_____

_____

_____

_____

_____

_____

MegaSkills Moments: The Last Year

If your child is in day care or preschool, think back over the last year. Ask yourself, "To what extent did I do any of the following?"

During the Last Year, I...	Once	More Than Once
Participated in a conference at preschool to discuss my child's progress and program.		
Attended PTA, Back to School, or a similar meeting at school.		
Served as a volunteer at school.		
Attended a school concert or other event.		
Talked with a teacher informally and/or socially.		
Contacted other parents or a community group on behalf of the school and educational issues.		
Other:		

Notes to myself: _____

_____

_____

_____

_____

_____

_____

_____

_____

_____

_____

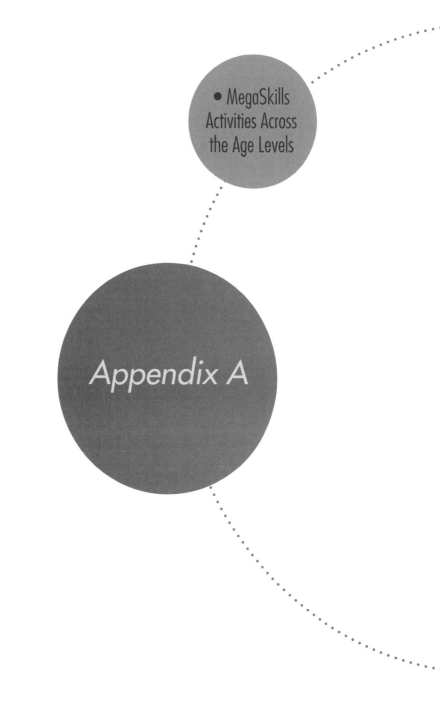

• MegaSkills
Activities Across
the Age Levels

Appendix A

MegaSkills Activities Across the Age Levels

Each chapter lists the activities for the MegaSkill in the specific age level. This Grid shows the MegaSkills across age levels.

For example, when you are looking for activities to build your child's confidence, find your child's age, check the page numbers indicated below and select the activities.

When you want more "recipes," check the activities in the adjacent ages. Children develop on their own individual schedules, so activities from different age ranges can also be appropriate.

MEGASKILLS	Starting Out Ages: 1–2	Keeping Going Ages: 2–3	Sailing Along Ages: 2–3	Moving Forward Ages: 3–4	Taking Big Steps Ages: 4–5	Opening Schools Doors Ages: 5–6
CONFIDENCE	32, 33	50, 51, 52	78, 79, 80	110, 111, 112	145, 146, 147	181, 182, 184
MOTIVATION	34	53, 54	81, 82, 83	113, 114	148, 149, 150	185, 186
EFFORT	35	55, 56	84, 85	115, 116, 117	151, 152	186, 187, 188
RESPONSIBILITY	36	57	86, 87	118, 119, 120, 121	153, 154, 155	189, 190, 191
INITIATIVE	37	58, 59	88, 89, 90	122, 123, 124	156, 157, 158	192, 193, 194
PERSEVERANCE	38	60, 61, 62	91	125, 126	159, 160	195, 196
CARING	39	64	92, 93	126, 127	161, 162	197, 198, 199
TEAMWORK	40	65, 66, 67	94, 95	128, 129, 130	164, 165, 166	200, 201, 202
COMMON SENSE	41	68, 69	96, 97	131, 132, 133	166, 167, 168	203, 204, 205, 206
PROBLEM SOLVING	42, 43	70	97, 98, 99, 100	134, 135	169, 170, 171	207, 208, 209, 210
FOCUS	44	71, 72	101, 102, 103	136, 137	172, 173, 174	211, 212
RESPECT	45, 46	73, 74	104, 105	138, 139, 140	175, 176	213, 214, 215, 216

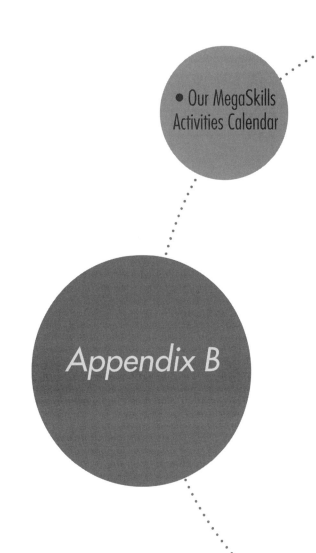

• Our MegaSkills
Activities Calendar

Appendix B

Our MegaSkills Activities Calendar

This calendar is a reminder to do the MegaSkills activities. Post it in a place where everyone can see it. Make duplicates of this blank page so you can use it again. Keep your filled-in pages as a record of progress.

ACTIVITY NAME	DATE TO DO ACTIVITY	COMMENTS: DID WE LIKE IT?

TIPS FOR PARENTS

- Mark your calendar to make sure you remember to do the activity with your child.

- Pick the time of day you like best to do the activity together.

- First read the entire activity carefully.

- Don't worry about doing anything wrong.

- Start the activity by saying. "Let's do it."

- Don't expect a perfect job.

- Use the activities as beginnings.

- Use your own imagination. Ask your child for ideas.

- Create your own new activities together.

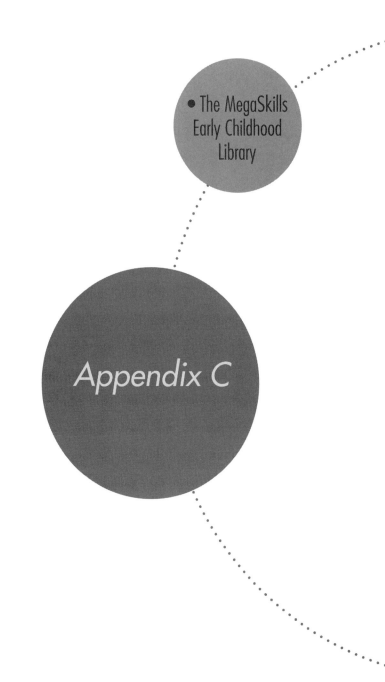

The MegaSkills
Early Childhood
Library

Appendix C

• The MegaSkills Early Childhood Library

Children's books abound in MegaSkills, but you have to know where to look to find them. In this appendix are age-old classics as well as books published within the last few years. This brief list is only a starting point. The lists include titles across the age spectrum for babies, toddlers, and preschoolers. It is fine to read "younger" or "older" books aloud with your child—select books that appeal to you and your child.

Books for Very Young Children

Even when children chew on the books as you read to them, keep reading. That's the word from educators and language experts across the world. Here are five classic board books for little ones

Brown Bear, Brown Bear, What Do You See? by Bill Martin Jr., illustrated by Eric Carle.

Pat the Bunny by Edith Kunhardt Davies.

Goodnight Moon by Margaret Wise Brown, illustrated by Clement Hurd.

The Very Hungry Caterpillar by Eric Carle.

The Tale of Peter Rabbit by Beatrix Potter.

Growing Up with Books

The following books have been identified by librarians as having special significance in support of MegaSkills. Thanks to the libraries of the District of Columbia and to the Enoch Pratt Free Library, Baltimore, Maryland, for helping develop these lists. Special thanks to Ellen Riordan, Children's Services Coordinator at Enoch Pratt, for the newest selections for the youngest children.

Read books together. Listen to your child read; let your child listen to you read. Talk about the books, enjoy them, and let them become part of your lives. Let the power of literature reinforce and extend your child's MegaSkills, building imagination and a love of reading.

CONFIDENCE

Brown, Margaret Wise. *Runaway Bunny.*

Chodos-Irvine, Margaret. *Ella Sarah Gets Dressed.*

Falconer, Ian. *Olivia.*

Lester, Helen. *Tacky the Penguin.*

Lloyd-Jones, Sally. *How to Be a Baby, By Me, The Big Sister.*

Waddell, Martin. *The Tough Princess.*

Waddell, Martin. *Owl Babies.*

Weeks, Sarah. *Overboard.*

Weiss, Nicki. *Battle Day at Camp Belmont.*

MOTIVATION

Carle, Eric. *The Very Quiet Cricket.*

Cohen, Miriam. *When Will I Read?*

Freschet, Bernice. *Furlie Cat.*

Henkes, Kevin. *Kitten's First Full Moon.*

Katz, Karen. *Counting Kisses.*

Kubler, Annie. *If You're Happy And You Know It…*

Sage, James. *Farmer Smart's Fat Cat.*

EFFORT

Kubler, Annie. *Head, Shoulders, Knees and Toes…*

Slater, Dashka. *Baby Shoes.*

Smith, Maggie. *One Naked Baby: Counting to Ten and Back Again.*

RESPONSIBILITY

Boynton, Sandra. *The Going to Bed Book.*

Chodos-Irvine, Margaret. *Ella Sarah Gets Dressed.*

Fox, Mem. *Time for Bed.*

Zion, Gene. *The Plant Sitter.*

INITIATIVE

Barton, Byron. *I Want to Be an Astronaut*.

Elya, Susan Middleton. *Bebe Goes Shopping*.

McKissack, Patricia. *Flossie and the Fox*.

Paterson, John, and Katherine Paterson. *Blueberries for the Queen*.

Patricelli, Leslie. *Binky*.

Uchida, Yoshiko. *Sumi's Prize*.

PERSEVERANCE

Boutis, Victoria. *Katy Did It*.

Graham, Thomas. *Mr. Bear's Chair*.

Henkes, Kevin. *Kitten's First Full Moon*.

Hubbell, Patricia. *Wrapping Paper Romp*.

Martin, Bill Jr. *Chicka Chicka Boom Boom*.

CARING

Allen, Jonathan. *I Am Not Cute*.

Asch, Frank. *Moon Bear*.

Bang, Molly. *Ten, Nine, Eight*.

Boynton, Sandra. *Snuggle Puppy*.

Moss, Miriam. *Don't Forget I Love You*.

Oxenbury, Helen. *Mother's Helper*.

Ryan, Pam Munoz. *Mice and Beans*.

Ryder, Joanne. *Bear of My Heart*.

Simont, Marc. *The Stray Dog*.

TEAMWORK

Burningham, John. *Mr. Gumpy's Motor Car*.

Domanska, Janina. *The Turnip*.

Ernst, Lisa Campbell. *Squirrel Park*.

Fox, Mem. *Shoes from Grandpa*.

Ginsburg, Mirra. *Mushrooms in the Rain*.

Mills, Lauren. *The Rag Coat.*
Rathman, Peggy. *Good Night Gorilla.*
Rohman, Eric. *My Friend Rabbit.*
Seeger, Laura Vaccaro. *Dog and Bear.*
Steptoe, John. *Baby Says.*

COMMON SENSE

Asch, Frank. *Turtle Tale.*
Boynton, Sandra. *Moo Baa La La La.*
Hoban, Tana. *Black on White.*
LaFontaine, Jean de. *The Miller, the Boy and the Donkey.*
Paul, Galdone. *Little Red Hen.*
Shaw, Charles G. *It Looked Like Spilt Milk.*
Waber, Bernard. *A Lion Named Shirley Williamson.*

PROBLEM SOLVING

Brown, Margaret Wise. *Once Upon a Time in a Pigpen.*
Butler, John. *Whose Nose and Toes?*
Hong, Lily Toy. *Two of Everything.*
Siomades, Lorianne. *Itsy Bitsy Spider.*
Steig, William. *Abel's Island.*
Willems, Mo. *Knuffle Bunny: A Cautionary Tale.*

FOCUS

McCloskey, Robert. *Make Way for Ducklings.*
Oxenbury, Helen. *All Fall Down.*
Oxenbury, Helen. *Clap Hands.*
Reiser, Lynn. *You and Me, Baby.*
Zion, Gene. *The Plant Sitter.*

RESPECT

Andree, Giles. *Giraffes Can't Dance.*

De Regniers, Beatrice Schenk. *May I Bring a Friend?*

Kraus, Robert. *Leo the Late Bloomer.*

Meyers, Susan. *Everywhere Babies.*

Seeger, Laura Vaccaro. *Dog and Bear.*

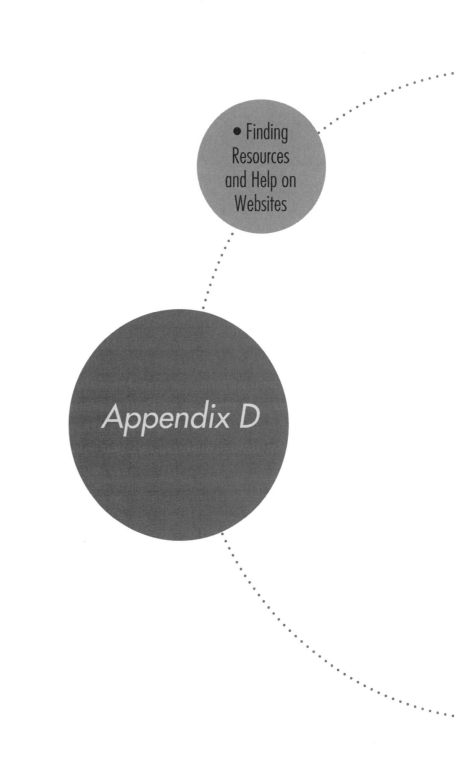

- Finding Resources and Help on Websites

Appendix D

Websites

For many of us, not having family near us to guide our parenting is a personal loss. Yet, there is more information (more than we may know what to do with) on the Web and in our own local communities. This does not make up for family, but it does provide us with a wide, wide world of information. This is a starter list. New sites are started every day and some leave the Web, so check your favorites often.

Parenting and Parent Education

Brazelton Institute—www.brazelton-institute.com
Bright Futures—www.brightfutures.aap.org
Family Support Network—www.familysupportnet.org
Home Program for Preschool Youngsters—www.hippyusa.org
MegaSkills Education Center—www.megaskills.org, www.dorothyrich.net
National Parent Information Network—www.npin.org
Newborns—www.parenttime.com
Parenthood.com—www.parenthood.com
Parenting-qa.com—www.parenting-qa.com
Parent News—www.parent.net.
Parents as Teachers—www.patnc.org
Parents Place—www.parentsplace.com
Parents Place (ivillage)—www.parenting.ivillage.com
Parents Services Project—www.parentservices.org
Parent Soup—www.familyfirst.com/parent_soup
PBS—www.pbsparents.org and www.pbskids.org
Sesame Workshop—www.sesameworkshop.org
Zero to Three—www.zerotothree.org

Literacy and Reading

America Reads—www.americareads.com
International Reading Association—www.reading.org
National Center of Family Literacy—www.famlit.org
Public Library Association—www.pla.org

Reach Out and Read—www.reachoutandread.org
Reading is Fundamental—www.rif.org
Scholastic Publishers—www.scholastic.com
WETA LD Online and Reading Rockets—www.ldonline.org
WGBH Between the Lions—www.pbskids.org/lions

News and Current Events Affecting Children

Administration for Children Families—www.acf.hhs.gov
American Academy of Pediatrics—www.aap.org
Children First—www.children-first.org
Children's Defense Fund—www.childrensdefense.org
Connect For Kids—www.connectkids.org
Education Week on the Web—www.edweek.org
National Children's Coalition—www.child.net
National Council of La Raza—www.nclr.org
News in Education—www.newsineducation.com
Pre-K Now—www.preknow.org
Public Agenda: Policies and Issues—www.publicagenda.org
School of the 21st Century—www.yale.edu/21c
U.S. Department of Education/America Goes Back to School—
    www.ed.gov or 1-800-USA-LEARN

Mommy Blogs: Interactive, Entertaining, and Helpful

There are more websites out there, some starting new every day. You will find them in your searches. You have to start somewhere. These are great places to begin.
Clubmom.com—www.clubmom.com
Consolidated list of mommy/women's blogs—www.blogher.org
Cool Mom Picks—www.coolmompicks.com
Father's Network—www.mrdad.com
General Parenting—www.kidssource.com
Mocha Moms—www.mochamoms.org
Modern Mom—www.modernmom.com/site/home.php

Mommy Track'd—www.mommytrackd.com

Momready.com—www.momready.com

MV Parents—www.mvparents.com

Parent Sharing—www.Mayasmom.com

SheFindsMom—www.shefindsmom.com/index.php

Sharing Experiences over 40 TeeBeeDee—www.tbd.com

Special Learning Needs

Easter Seals—www.easter-seals.org

International Dyslexia Association—www.interdys.org

Learning Disabilities Association of America—www.ldaamerica.org

National Center for Learning Disabilities—www.ncld.org

National Dissemination Center for Children with Disabilities—www.nichcy.org

National Institute of Child Health & Human Development—www.nichd.nih.gov

Share Your Favorites

Each of us has favorite books and websites. Let us know about your favorites, and we'll share news of your picks on our website with parents across the nation and the world. Send email to edstaff@megaskills.hsi.org.

The Internet is not the only place to check for answers to your questions. Remember the local library, health, recreation, and child care centers. With the increased attention being given to the need for preschool education for all children, many local centers now offer materials for parents that were not previously available.

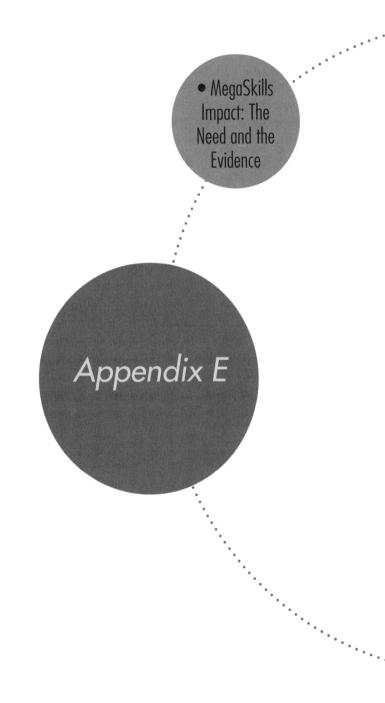

● MegaSkills
Impact: The
Need and the
Evidence

Appendix E

• MegaSkills Impact: The Need and the Evidence

Adults need not be graduates of fancy colleges or have high incomes to be able to help children learn. Every caregiver is a teacher, every day is learning time, and every place is a learning place.

Thinking this way is not designed to create little Einsteins. It is designed to create learners. Our children will live in an ever more demanding and volatile world. Today's children need beyond-the-basics capacities for continuing to learn and to adapt to the changes that will be part of their everyday lives.

Parents and teachers have been sharing their experiences with us over the years. Here are just a few. First, there are heartfelt comments. For the evaluation data, see the studies that follow. MegaSkills has proven to be a winner for children, families, and teachers.

Parents' Experiences

"MegaSkills has been a lifesaver for our whole family. The practical, positive information has allowed us to work together with more harmony and peacefulness."

"My husband and I were at odds much of the time in regard to child discipline. MegaSkills gave us a happy medium. Communication between us has never been better, and communication with our children is more open."

"We have never been to the library so often as we have this year." A mother reports that her child says to her, "Oh, Mommy, this is so good."

"Grandparents have more time to give to children. I worked with four children using this program. Each one wanted to get involved, to give ideas. It gave them confidence. There's a whole group of grandparents out there who have no idea of how important they are in the education of children."

"I'm seeing that my parenting skills match other parents, GADS! I'm doing something right. I've learned better what to apply, what I know and feel and think—even for myself, not just for my child."

"Not only does MegaSkills advise us to teach children fundamental skills. It tells me HOW to teach. It's not an overnight accomplishment, but it is the next best thing. MegaSkills gives clear, precise activities to do with your child on a normal person's schedule. I have found it relieves the guilt associated with not spending enough quality time with children. It tells you what to do with them. It's so simple. I wonder why I didn't think of it."

MegaSkills Evaluations

Memphis State University researchers, evaluating the impact on families participating in the MegaSkills Workshop Program in Tennessee, found:

- Children spending six hours a week on homework doubled to 24 percent from 12 percent.

- Average time children spent watching TV during the school week decreased thirty-one minutes per week. Time not spent on TV was spent on homework.

- Average time parents spent with children each day increased after the workshops to 2.25 hours from 2.02 hours.

Austin Independent School District, Austin, Texas, using the MegaSkills Leader Program tracked 1196 students in grades preK to six and found students whose parents attended MegaSkills Workshops showed:

- Higher scores on statewide achievement tests

- Higher attendance rates

- Fewer discipline problems

- Higher test scores than the national average

Appeal for younger learners and older learners: These recipes provide verbal and action opportunities. Young children often find it easier to speak through drawings. Older children benefit from discussions.

Consistency of format: The recipe "system" helps to establish children's expectations, security, and positive anticipation.

Current research supports the work of MegaSkills. Among the findings from the Educational Testing Service report: "The Family: America's Smallest School" (2008):

"It's understandable that education reform would focus on improving schools… however we will have to go far beyond this focus if we hope to significantly improve student learning and reduce the achievement gap. If we are to improve America's academic standing within the global community, and close our all-too-persistent achievement gaps, we must help assure nurturing home environments and supportive, encouraging family lives for all our children."

For more information, please visit:

www.ets.org
  The Family: America's Smallest School

www.wholechildeducation.org
  Whole Child Resolution Toolkit

www.CASEL.org
  Social and Emotional Learning for Student Success

• With Special
Thanks To...

Acknowledgments

"All of us have
moments in our childhood
where we come alive for
the first time. And we go
back to those moments
and think, This is when I
became myself."
— Rita Dove, poet

"Go younger"—that is the message we heard from parents across the nation and abroad. We have responded to the message with this new book, *MegaSkills for Babies, Toddlers, and Beyond.*

Research has been clear that the early years before school are critical determiners for children's achievement. MegaSkills has been unique in its impact at the school age years. Now, MegaSkills activities are available to families and teachers for children starting at age one.

Thanks go to Dorothy's grandsons, Nathan and Nicky Baron. Dorothy has been involved with their growth and development since their birth. She has adapted and field-tested MegaSkills activities for them throughout their toddler and pre-school years.

Thanks to the preschoolers, and to teacher Tracy Berry and Pastor Donna Hinkle, who tested MegaSkills activities that Beverly adapted for her church preschool.

And thanks to a multinational milk products company which wanted to place MegaSkills activities on their cans of formula for very young children. This request prompted us to move forward and complete MegaSkills for the Early Years. It is often from serendipitous experiences that major breakthroughs are launched. Bringing MegaSkills activities to families wherever they can be reached throughout the community continues to be the hope and a plan for both of us.

Our continuing thanks go to our husbands, Spencer Rich and Tony Mattox, and to Beverly's stepfather, Frank, for patience, encouragement, and good ideas. Between us, we have four daughters and three sons-in-law—Rebecca, Jessica and Jon, Leanne and Gary, Leslie and Dave—now grown, who are making their way in the wide world. Their MegaSkills work for them everyday.

To Tess Sartin, Administrative Assistant, who deciphers our handwriting and makes sure that we reach out and respond to communities nationally.

To Peter Lynch and Sara Appino of Sourcebooks, Lisa Queen and Eleanor Jackson of Queen Literary Agency, who saw the need for this book, and who made it possible.

To the librarians at the Enoch Pratt Free Library in Baltimore (Carla Hayden and Ellen Riordan) for the early childhood books in this edition and to the District of Columbia Library (Maria Salvadore and Pam Stovall) for their book lists from the earlier editions.

To the leadership, the Board and Advisors of the Home and School Institute, and to foresighted school districts, businesses, and community organizations that have taken important pioneering steps in supporting the MegaSkills programs. They range from small cities to large ones in forty-eight states, from Alaska to Georgia, from California to Vermont. Thanks to the John D. and Catherine T. MacArthur Foundation for funding the initial New Partnerships in Student Achievement Program, in which the MegaSkills activities were piloted.

To Harriett Stonehill, MegaSkills Education Director, who led the initiative to bring MegaSkills workshops to schools nationally and abroad and to all who have become MegaSkills leaders and MegaSkills Field Associates. There is no way to keep up and mention everyone on this great honor roll—but we know you. This is a diverse group working with thousands of teachers, parents, grandparents, and businesses across the nation, in a variety of settings, from schools to work places to housing centers.

We are appreciative of the work of early education advocates and researchers we deeply respect, among them: T. Berry Brazelton, Bettye Caldwell, Rudolf Dreikurs, Marian Wright Edelman, David Elkind, Erik Erikson, Selma Fraiberg, Ellen Galinsky, Haim Ginott, Stanley Greenspan, Jane Healy, Marguerite Kelly, Maria Montessori, Jean Piaget, Marilyn Segal, and Edward Zigler.

The period between the publication of the original *MegaSkills* in 1988 and this edition has been a time of learning for us. We had not imagined the power of the MegaSkills concept and how important and useful it would become for so many families and teachers.

Bringing this new knowledge together for this new book has been a challenge and a great joy. We have been taught by many fine teachers, parents, and children who are using MegaSkills, and we are grateful.

About the Authors

Dorothy Rich, EdD, is founder and president of the nonprofit Home and School Institute (HSI), based in Washington, DC. An acclaimed expert in family educational involvement, Dr. Rich is the author of the original MegaSkills publications and the developer of the MegaSkills training programs, used by more than four thousand schools across the United States and abroad. In her lifetime of work in the field, she has focused on helping families and educators team together to build achievement in school and beyond.

In honor of the twentieth anniversary of the original MegaSkills edition, Dr. Rich has launched five new initiatives: MegaSkills Site Awards; MegaSkills Leader Corps; MegaSkills for Children's Health; the book *MegaSkills*; and the book *Getting Along for the Sake of the Kids: What Parents and Teachers Really Need To Survive and Thrive in Today's Schools.*

Dorothy Rich's work has received the A+ for Breaking the Mold Award from the U.S. Department of Education, as well as recognition from the MacArthur Foundation and other distinguished foundations. Her work has been researched, tested, and found to be effective in raising student achievement, decreasing discipline problems, increasing time spent on homework, and decreasing time spent watching TV. Her work has been featured in the *Washington Post,* the *New York Times,* the *Los Angeles Times,* NBC's *Today, Education Week,* ABC's *Good Morning America,* and *Reader's Digest.*

Beverly Mattox, MEd, an active educator for over fifty years, has served as a teacher, principal, project director, and training specialist. She has collaborated with Dorothy Rich since 1972. As a speaker and workshop leader, she has conducted programs for school systems and organizations in twenty-six states and Canada. Two of her special interests are parenting and women's friendships. She has addressed more than four hundred groups and has completed doctoral course work in the areas of curriculum supervision and family counseling. She has served as an adjunct professor for four colleges, as a reviewer for the *Journal of Staff Development,* and contributor to the Standards for Staff Development.

Beverly authored *Getting It Together*, a primer for understanding Kohlberg's theory of cognitive moral development, and co-authored with Dorothy Rich *101 Activities for School-Community Involvement.* She serves on the board of directors of Agape Inc., an organization that services the needs of young mothers and their children.

Beverly is very active in her church and heads the "Especially for You" project, which collects and distributes needed items to the abused and homeless. She was recognized as a Jefferson Award winner on Delmarva for her work.

• *Join the New MegaSkills Network*

More and more MegaSkills participants have asked for ways to keep in touch and build support and encouragement for our work. Sign up at the new website www.dorothyrich.net. It is all about our new publications and offers a number of special features.

Free Benefits of Joining the MegaSkills Network

- Reduced costs for Network members for new books signed by the authors.
- Access to a complete book discussion guide and articles to reprint and share with others.
- The MegaSkills song, *Music and Lyrics*
- Opportunities for Network members to contribute to the site

Join today by completing the membership form on www.dorothyrich.net.

Our basic site, www.megaskills.org, will continue with a special focus for educators and also on our Institute publications.

Five No-Cost Steps You Can Take Now to Support MegaSkills

1. Go to www.dorothyrich.net to sign up as a MegaSkills Network member.
2. Write a brief Amazon.com review of MegaSkills (a few words will do) or write about MegaSkills on your favorite blogs.
3. Talk up and share MegaSkills with others. Contact us and we will send you materials for your presentation.
4. If you would like to be involved in helping to sell the books, let us know of your interest.
5. Keep your notes and letters coming … and we'll post them on the website.

• Announcing a New MegaSkills Website: www.dorothyrich.net

Beverly Mattox and Dorothy Rich invite you to visit the website and discover recipes for building our children's character and achievement in school and in life.

The new editions of MegaSkills are unlike any other parenting/education books. They combine character education at home with readiness for academic achievement at school. This new website (www.dorothyrich.net) includes sample activities from the new books, articles that can be reprinted, a complete discussion book club guide, and the new MegaSkills song. Visit the website often. There's a lot to share. Tell your friends about it!

What you'll find on the new website:

- The MegaSkils song, *Music and Lyrics*

- The new and complete MegaSkills Book Discussion Guide

- Tables of contents, reviews and sample activities from the two new editions of MegaSkills

The website was designed by IT specialist Kathy Murdock, of the Fort Belvoir Elementary School, Fairfax, Virginia, and the new MegaSkills song was written by singer/songwriter Lois Morton. The MegaSkills song CD with music will be available soon. Contact www.dorothyrich.net.

The basic MegaSkills website www.megaskills.org continues as a great resource for MegaSkills books, bilingual materials and posters.

• *The MegaSkills Book Discussion Guide*

This new guide is ideal for parent meetings and group discussions on education and parenting. It totals twenty-nine pages and is available free to MegaSkills Network members only at www.dorothyrich.net

The MegaSkills Book Discussion Guide is designed to help each of us think about our children's education and our role in building our children's MegaSkills. The questions raised in this guide cover a wide range of ages, from toddlers into the school years, and help children form a base of understanding that starts young and keeps going. Here are a few examples.

CONFIDENCE

Asking Ourselves

What recent good thing helped give me more confidence?

What less-than-good thing happened recently? How did it affect my confidence?

What do I remember about my own confidence when I was growing up?

Reminding Ourselves: When we feel hurt, we may think, "No one else has ever felt this way." Children may say, "You'll never understand." That's why our children need to know that adult confidence has ups and downs, too.

———

RESPECT

Asking Ourselves

How are we actively building our children's respect for family and community, so that children themselves, as they grow, are able to answer questions such as these:

How do I want my friends and family to be proud of me, to respect me?

Am I accepting of other people who are different from me?

Reminding Ourselves: We enjoy give and take with our children, not for nasty "talk-back" but to encourage expression that respects the rights of others and ourselves. We need to realize that our children have experiences and even some knowledge that they need to share, and we need to listen.

———————

AS PARENTS, AS TEACHERS, wanting the best for our children, we're together in the same boat together on a vast ocean. We can all use help in rowing the boat across.

For the complete guide, see www.dorothyrich.net.